BY PETER FARB

Illustrations by Kazue Mizumura

the story of
BUTTERFLIES
and other Insects

 HARVEY HOUSE, PUBLISHERS • *Irvington-on-Hudson, New York*

Library of Congress Catalog Card No.: 59-14884

Contents

Foreword

The writing of a science book is always a collaboration. The author whose name appears on the title page has merely brought together the facts accumulated by hundreds of scientists. Therefore, I should like to thank my unknown collaborators: the entomologists who have enriched my knowledge of the fascinating insects.

I am particularly grateful to Dr. Asher Treat of the College of the City of New York, Past President of the New York Entomological Society, who spent many hours critically reading my manuscript and making helpful suggestions to improve its accuracy.

To the others who have assisted me in the course of writing this book, I owe gratitude: Mr. John Pallister and Mrs. Patricia Vaurie of the American Museum of Natural History, and Mr. Tony Roberts, President of the New York Junior Entomological Society.

I should like to dedicate this book to my two children, Mark and Tommy, and to thank them for their curiosity about the six-legged creatures with whom we share the globe.

PETER FARB

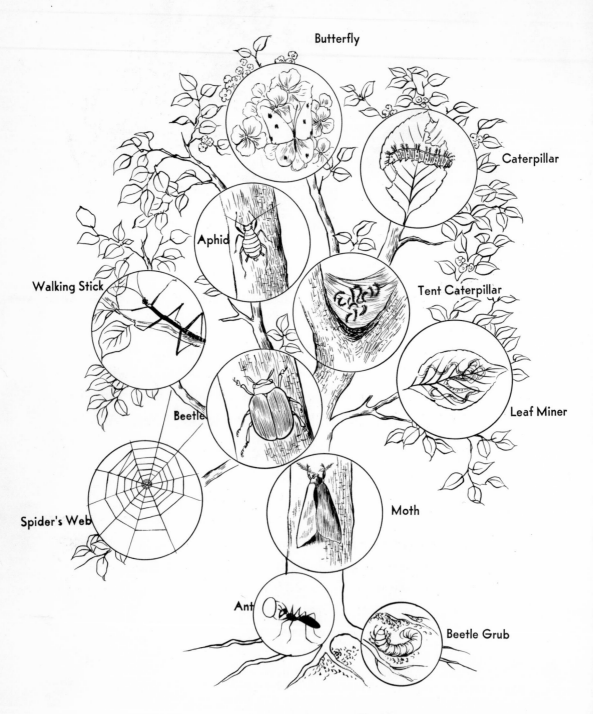

Insects Are Everywhere on a Shrub

1

The Insect Wonder World

Just as there was at one time an Age of Dinosaurs, so we today live in an Age of Insects. Insects are all around us, and practically every square inch of land harbors one type of insect, at least.

The Age of Insects

Explorers scaling the Himalaya Mountains have found insects living near the icy peaks. Other kinds of insects inhabit the mud of hot springs where the temperature often reaches 120°. One kind of fly can be found only in the pools of oil around the wells in southern California, and nowhere else!

The numbers of insects in the world are almost unbelievable. One scientist estimated that there were about 130,000,000 of them on a single acre of land that he had studied in Pennsylvania. Insects can increase their numbers so rapidly that in a single summer one pair of Houseflies could become the ancestors of 191,000,000,000,000,000,000 more flies! Of course, this would never happen, as flies could never multiply at this rapid rate. Other insects, birds, and a shortage of food would manage to lessen the population of these insects.

Entomologists (enn-toh-MOLL-oh-jists) are the scientists who specialize in the study of insects. Even they do not actually know how many different kinds of insects there are on the earth. The majority of entomologists, however, agree that the number is about 750,000 species (SPEE-sheez), or different kinds. That means that there are more than three times as many insect species as there are all the kinds of birds, mammals, fish, reptiles and other animals *combined!*

There may be more insect species in just one of their many groups than there are numbers of stars that you can see with the naked eye. If you should begin now to write the names of all the known insects, and if you worked day and night without a moment to rest or to eat, it would take you nearly six months to complete the task. If a museum owned just one specimen of every insect species, and then lined up all the specimens in single file, the parade would stretch for about eight miles.

Insects are able to endure many hardships. Some of them have been frozen at many degrees below zero, and others have been heated to high temperatures, yet they managed to survive. One Ladybird beetle was kept under water for more than a day but did not drown.

Because insects are so hardy and so numerous, one entomologist has said that insects will be the last form of animal life to survive on earth when the sun dies out.

Of course it will be millions of years before any such fate befalls our planet. That gives us plenty of time to study insects and to learn about their fascinating ways of life. Perhaps we may also discover their secrets for survival.

We who live in the United States and Canada share our land and air with about 85,000 different kinds of insects, and every one of them has an amazing life-history.

Strange Lives

In exploring the insect wonder world, you will meet strange creatures. Some kinds were born without mouths or stomachs; some have as many as 30,000 eyes. Some may look fearsome or odd, while many are as beautiful as a rainbow. Some insects use tear gas; others raise cattle; still others build giant cities and wage costly wars.

Among the largest insects is a beetle about 4½ inches long. It is so large that entomologists have named it the "Goliath beetle," after the giant with whom David, the shepherd boy in the Bible, fought. The Goliath beetle wears horns on its head. It uses these horns for stripping the bark of trees so that it can

reach the sweet sap underneath. It also finds the horns perfect tools for peeling bananas. The smallest insect is also a beetle, but it is so tiny that it could fly through the eye of a sewing needle.

The common insects now found in any back yard or city park performed amazing feats millions of years before man was able to do the same things. The first "musician" on Earth may have been the cricket. The first "manufacturer" of paper was probably a wasp. One of the first creatures to use silk was a caterpillar.

Insects have discovered more different ways of living than has any other group of animals. How did they manage to do this? First of all, insects are a very ancient form of life. They have had millions of years in which to change. If we were magically transported to the Age of Dinosaurs, everything might look strange to us, but there would still be insects around. We would still have to swat mosquitoes, but on the other hand we could also admire the colorful butterflies.

There is another reason for the marvelous variety of shapes and habits we find in the insect clan. An insect has hundreds of generations in which to change during the time that it takes a human baby to grow into an adult. Consequently, any improvement is rapidly passed on to the insect children. Scientists call this development *evolution* (ev-oh-LEW-shun). Every form of life has evolved from some older, and often simpler, form. Insects, however, seem to have developed faster than many other animals.

Very few insects are pests. It is true that some destroy our food and our possessions and even attack us. But most of them are harmless, and many are useful. You will learn quickly which insects are apt to sting or bite, and also how to take proper precautions. (I was never stung while examining wasp or bee nests. The only sting I ever received was while I was asleep on a chair outdoors!)

Every insect has a role to play in the world of nature. In a later chapter, we shall see how the life of a lowly insect may be tied to the lives of many other living creatures.

Insect Safari

The strange world of the insects is open for study to anyone with sharp eyes and a little patience. Wherever you live, you will find insects in your back yard or in a near by park or field. One entomologist found over 1000 species of insects in his tiny back yard. A butterfly collector netted eighty-five kinds of rainbow-hued butterflies at his home in the heart of New York City!

Insects are all around you. Go to the nearest shrub or tree and you will find insects chewing on the leaves. You may even see tiny insects actually living *inside* the thin leaves. Insects clamber over twigs and branches, or drill holes in the bark of trees to lay their eggs. Moths, butterflies, bees and wasps visit the flowers. Ants nest at the base of the tree trunk, and if you should dig down to the roots you would find many more insects living there.

I once timed myself to see how many different kinds of insects I could find on a small shrub in five minutes. When the five minutes were up, I had already counted nineteen species. Given more time, that number undoubtedly could have been doubled or tripled.

An explorer visiting Africa does not see stranger sights than you can witness in your back-yard jungle. When you stalk insects, trap them, keep them in your own insect zoo, you are really going on a voyage of exploration to a strange land. Many entomologists claim that much of the insect world is as un-explored as is darkest Africa.

What does a particular insect eat? Where does it live? What is its behavior? Perhaps in the case of the majority of insects, even these facts are not known. At the end of this book, hints are given on how you can keep insects and watch the marvels of their lives unfold.

Like any explorer departing for a strange land, you must first learn something about the animals you are going to hunt. But what makes an insect an insect?

2

What Is An Insect?

Ants are usually easy to find, so let us look closely at one through a magnifying glass to see why it is a member of the group of animals called Insects.

An ant has six jointed legs, as have all other insects. Spiders have more than six legs, so they are *not* insects. The ant's body consists of three parts: (1) a head, (2) a thorax or chest, and (3) an abdomen.

Each of these parts is separated by a narrow waist—and that is how the word "insect" is derived. "Insect" in Latin means "cut into," or "notched." It is very easy to find the thin waist in an ant or a wasp. The waists are not quite so easily seen in grasshoppers and some other insects, but if you look carefully, you will find that these insects also have their bodies notched into three parts.

Only insects have six legs and three sections to their bodies. But there are other facts about insects which we should also know. Insects do not have bones, as do people. Instead, they wear hard skeletons on the *outside* of their bodies, as if they had been turned inside out. This outer skeleton is somewhat like a coat of mail that a knight wore when he went into battle.

Before an insect is ready to shed its outer skeleton, it merely grows a larger one that is folded up underneath the outer one. Then the old skeleton splits open, and the insect walks out of it, wearing its larger skeleton. This process is called "molting," and an insect may grow a new coat a dozen times during its lifetime.

If we suspect that a creature as remarkable as an insect does not breathe the way a person does, we would be right. Instead of taking in air through its mouth, an insect breathes through tiny, pinprick openings, called *spiracles* (SPY-ruh-kullz), on both sides of its body.

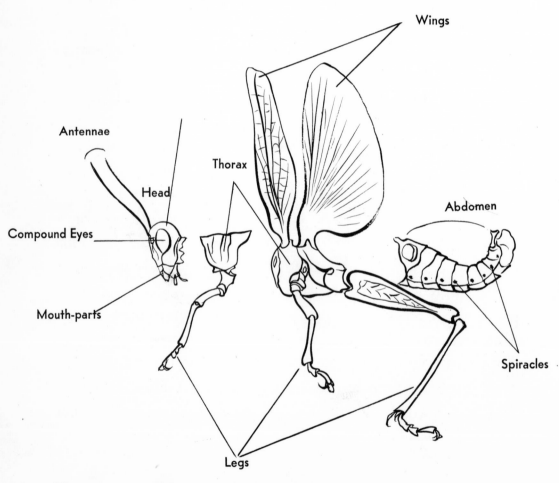

Anatomy of a Grasshopper

Nor would we be able very quickly to recognize an insect's brain, for an insect actually has several brains. Your own brain is like a broadcasting station that sends messages to all parts of your body by means of delicate wires or nerves. At various points along an insect's body, its nerves are grouped together into very small broadcasting stations. The various nerve bundles—or, as the entomologists would say, *ganglia,* (from a Greek word that means "swellings")—seem to control different activities. For example, an ant may lose its entire head in a battle with another ant, yet it can still climb and run. The remaining ganglia in the ant's body keep it alive until the insect finally dies of starvation.

Every mature insect has a pair of *antennae* (an-TEN-ee), or "feelers," that often resemble the "rabbit ears" on television sets. The antennae of an insect, however, are much more wonderful and sensitive than the mechanical ones, and are often made up of hundreds of parts. For some insects, the two antennae carry out the combined jobs of ears, nose, tongue and hands. These feelers allow some insects to find their way inside nests in the soil, where not even a flicker of light is available. Some use their feelers to taste their food and to detect sound vibrations.

No matter how carefully we try to sneak up on a Housefly, it almost always manages to take flight before we can catch it. The sight of an approaching hand does not warn the fly. Rather, the fly's antennae can feel the sudden, invisible stirring of the air caused by the moving hand.

An ant rushing across the ground usually travels a highway used as well by other ants. There are no signs visible on this highway, however. Instead, the ant's sensitive antennae detect odor markers that lead it back to its nest or to the foraging grounds.

Entomologists have proved this fact by placing dark wax over an ant's eyes as a blindfold. When the ant was put back on the trail, it hastened home just as it had been doing before it was blindfolded.

Then the scientists captured the same ant once again; this time they snipped off its antennae. As a result, it could no longer find the correct route, and it became lost. Thus the entomologists proved that ants usually use their antennae and not their eyes for following their trails. It is no wonder then that ants seem to spend so much time cleaning their very useful antennae.

A Few of the Thousands of Lenses (greatly magnified) in an Insect's Eyes

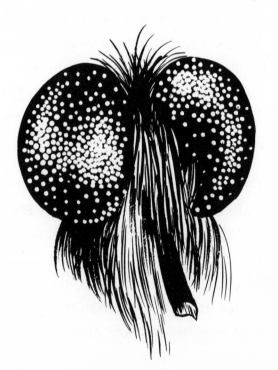

An Insect's Large Compound Eyes

The antennae of an insect are attached to the head between two large eyes. If you look at one of these eyes through a magnifying glass, you can easily see why they are called compound eyes. Each eye is actually made up of thousands of smaller eyes, as many as 15,000 of them in a Dragonfly.

Insect Tool Chests

Insects have not evolved the ability of making their own tools as we do. Instead, the tools are built right into the bodies of the insects.

The mouth-parts of insects act as precision tools for performing many tasks. Hornets and other paper-making wasps have mouth-parts like files. They use these files to scrape off tiny splinters of wood which they chew into pulp. A Leaf-cutting bee uses its jaws, as if they were scissors, to snip off circular bits of foliage. The mouth-parts of an ant, when they are closed, can work like a shovel and scoop out soil to build the nest.

Some insects have hollow needles on their heads with which they pierce a plant to suck the sweet sap. Only those insects that have hollow needles—such as Chinch bugs and Squash bugs—may be called "bugs." So, if you have been in the habit of calling every insect a bug, you know now that bugs form only one group of insects.

The three pairs of legs of an insect attend to many tasks that the mouth-parts are unable to perform. A Honeybee has baskets on its rear legs for carrying pollen from flowers back to the hive. A grasshopper's rear legs work like a catapult, and the legs of some water insects are shaped like rowing paddles.

19

In the strange world of insects, organs that are similar to ears are found on the legs of crickets. Many insects have a sense of taste located on their feet. One experiment with a butterfly revealed that its feet were 200 times as sensitive to sugar as are our tongues. A mosquito's front legs are sensitive to invisible heat waves given off by a human body. That is the reason a mosquito can accurately find its human target in a completely darkened room.

The Marvel of Wings

The thorax of an insect (that part of the body next to the head) is concerned with motion. Three pairs of legs are attached to the thorax, as are also the wings. The wings are amazingly strong, yet lightweight. A Honeybee's wings may beat 15,000 times a minute. A Dragonfly can zoom at speeds upwards of twenty-five miles an hour. In addition, it can fly backwards as well as forwards, and also hang suspended in mid-air like a helicopter. The strength of a Dragonfly's wings comes from the thousands of veins and struts that support them.

Wings also perform many other tasks for insects besides flying. Katydids and crickets rub their wings together to make music. Honeybees use their wings to air-condition the hive. During the cold winter, bees beat their wings, thus generating heat to warm the hive. In summer, the wings serve as fans to ventilate the hive.

Some of the earliest insects on earth, such as Dragonflies and Termites, have two pairs of wings, both pairs being approximately the same size and shape. But during the hundreds of millions of years in which insects have existed there has been ample time for them to evolve many different sorts of wings.

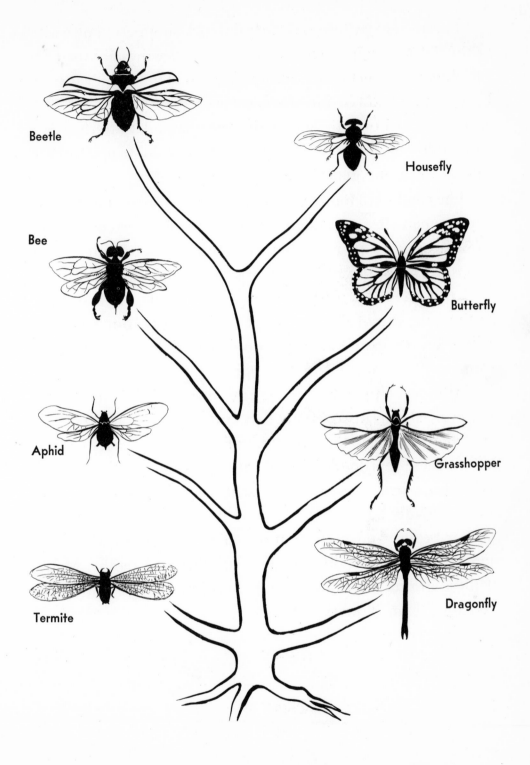

Beetle

Housefly

Bee

Butterfly

Aphid

Grasshopper

Termite

Dragonfly

Evolution of Insect Wings

The ancient pattern was altered by grasshoppers. The width of their front wings is reduced and the rear wings are used for lift. Beetles have further improvements. The front wings of beetles have evolved into hard covers which protect the rear wings when these are not in use. Moths and butterflies use still a different method. They lock together the wings on each side to form one giant wing.

The common Housefly and its relatives display the greatest improvement in insect flight. The rear wings are completely eliminated and a pair of vibrating knobs are substituted. The knobs work like balancers, or gyroscopes, to aid in steering.

Insects were the earliest fliers on the globe. At first, they had no enemies in the air except other insects. But here was a food source in the air that could not be ignored by other animals.

Millions of years later some tiny mammals learned to fly, and evolved into insect-eating bats. Similarly, in some reptiles, the front legs turned into wings, and through the ages of evolution, these reptiles developed into birds that pursue the insects. Birds, bats, and insects are still the only kinds of animal life that really fly.

For beauty and perfection of wings, one group of insects stands out above all others—the butterflies and moths. Many of these insects are so magnificently colored that a naturalist has called them "flowers that fly."

3

Beauty

Butterflies and Moths

Butterflies and moths wear glittering particles of dust on their wings. If you should hold one of these insects by the wings, you will notice that the colorful specks will brush off onto your finger tips like talcum powder. Under the microscope, these particles are seen to be tiny scales, fitted on the transparent wings in the same way as shingles on a house roof. That is why the scientific name for butterflies and moths is *Lepidoptera* (LEPP-ih-DOPP-terr-uh) which in Greek means "scale-winged."

Butterflies are day fliers, while most moths take wing only after dusk. There are about ten times as many species of moths as there are butterflies in the United States and Canada, but we rarely see them, because of moths' night-flying habits.

There are other ways to tell butterflies and moths apart. A moth's body is usually thick and hairy, quite unlike the tapering grace of a butterfly's body. And if you are still uncertain which is which, wait for the insect to land. A butterfly at rest holds its wings high over its body as if they were flags, but the moth usually lets them droop like a tent.

23

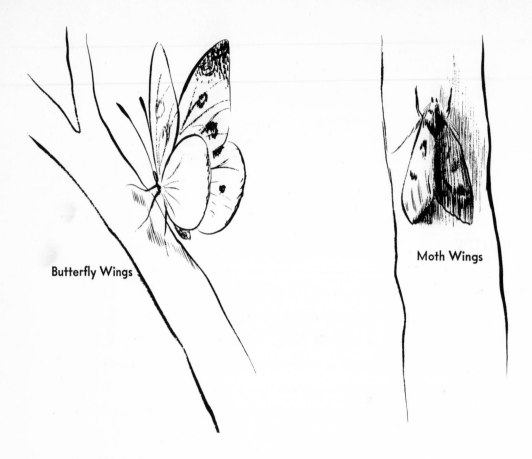

Butterfly Wings

Moth Wings

Butterflies take the awards for the most colorful wings, but butterflies' feelers cannot equal the beauty of the moths' antennae. Many moths have antennae that look like bird feathers or fern plants. The butterflies' antennae are plainer: they look like thin pieces of wire ending in little knobs.

Moth antennae are used primarily for finding food and a mate. Entomologists have performed many amazing experiments to see how sensitive the antennae are. For example, they have captured males and females of the same species and placed the females in an outdoor cage. They marked the males with paint on their wings, so that the moths could later be identified.

Then the entomologists took them great distances. When the males were set free, some sensed the odor of the females in the cages and promptly flew back to them. Males released more than a mile away have been known to return promptly to the cages of the females.

Most butterflies and some moths are as colorful as the flowers which they visit to sip nectar. But how do butterflies and moths reach the nectar deep inside the flowers? Instead of having a long bill like that of a hummingbird, these insects have long hollow tubes, like soda straws. In some species, their straws are six times as long as their bodies! You've probably never seen one of these tubes because the insects keep them rolled up under their heads when not in use. But when a butterfly or a moth lands on a blossom, it unrolls the soda straw to suck up the hidden sweets.

Some of the colorful butterflies use their bright markings to confuse their enemies. When these butterflies are pursued, they suddenly land and fold up their wings, thus revealing only the drab underside of their wings. This quick action and sudden hiding of their brilliant colors actually seem to make the butterflies disappear. Wings of the little Angle-wing butterflies often appear to be ripped and tattered, but these are really camouflaged wings—because when the Angle-wing falls to earth and lies still, it somewhat resembles a dead leaf.

The black-and-orange Monarch butterfly does not attempt to conceal itself. Its bright wings warn away bird enemies, for a Monarch is bitter to the taste. An inexperienced bird might attempt to eat a Monarch, but it will quickly toss the insect away in disgust. The bird, however, will remember the Monarch's color pattern and will not make the same mistake again.

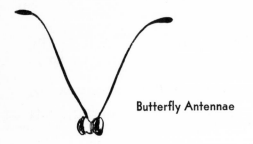

Butterfly Antennae

Moth Antennae

There is another butterfly, the Viceroy, that is a bluffer. Its coloring is almost exactly like that of the Monarch. The Viceroy lacks the bitter taste of the Monarch, but it mimics the latter so well that birds let the Viceroy alone, too.

Although butterflies appear to be frail and wispy, some kinds love a fight. They will strike each other sharply, rubbing off little puff bursts of scales; then they will zoom back and clash again. Rarely do they seriously hurt each other, however. Fights are usually between males of the same species, but butterflies have also been known to attack dogs, birds, and humans —harmlessly, of course.

One of the most warrior-like butterflies is the little Pearl Crescent. It carries on a lifelong feud with the much larger Buckeye, and attacks the Buckeye whenever one passes within range. The Pearl Crescent also annoys the Carolina locust, and beats at the locust unmercifully with its wings.

26

Some butterflies take long flights on their sturdy wings. One autumn, some people living on the island of Bermuda in the Atlantic Ocean noticed a black cloud approaching. When it came closer, the cloud was seen to be a mass of tiny yellow butterflies, Little Sulphurs, which soon dropped to earth to rest. The nearest land to Bermuda is more that 600 miles away —an amazing nonstop flight for such delicate insects.

Each spring clouds of Painted Lady butterflies migrate northwards from Mexico to California and the Southwestern states. One migration consisted of a solid mass of these butter-flies, about forty miles wide. It took three days to pass a given spot. There were probably about three *billion* Painted Lady butterflies in this one cloud—more butterflies than there are people on the Earth.

Rolled-up "Soda Straw" Tongue of Butterfly

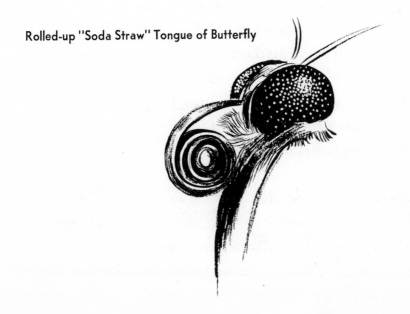

The Monarch, too, is a long-distance flier. It migrates from the northern states and Canada down to Mexico and Florida in the fall, just as many birds do. This best known of all our butterflies is as curious an insect as one is likely to find.

Mystery of the Monarch

As the cold days of autumn approach, the Monarch, king of the butterflies, no longer dances around the flowers searching for nectar. It clings to the branch of a tree, and soon it is joined by more Monarchs. Hordes of them form a sociable group that has put aside all thoughts of fighting. Suddenly, as if by some secret signal, they all fly from the tree and head southward for the winter—a journey of often thousands of miles.

One fall, in Pennsylvania, I watched a Monarch migration. It was far more astounding than the flight of the hawks which I had come 150 miles to see. The Monarchs drifted along in scattered flocks, sometimes only a foot off the ground, and rocked from side to side as they flew. They braved the winds and the rushing mountain air currents. I could not help admiring these brave insects, which were so light that perhaps a dozen of them would not equal the weight of a coin.

All along the southward route of the Monarchs are special resting places where they spend the night. These butterfly "motels," used each year by the Monarchs, are usually the trunks of trees. Tens of thousands of Monarchs may huddle together on a single branch. In the morning they fly off, following their invisible air highway to the next tree motel.

How do Monarchs manage to find the same trees year after year? Entomologists have observed unusual scales on the wings of male Monarchs. It is believed that these scales are scent glands which give out a butterfly perfume that is nearly odorless to us. Perhaps the perfume sticks to the tree trunks and, like an advertising billboard, tells the Monarchs when they have arrived at a good place to spend the night.

In the spring, the Monarchs return to the northern states. It is not certain whether these are the same butterflies that

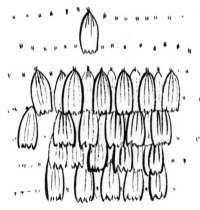

Scales on Butterfly Wings

Monarch Butterflies at Migration Time

went south in the fall, or if they are offspring born during the winter. The butterflies arrive in the north on tattered and dull wings. The female Monarch searches out the plants belonging to the milkweed family, and that family only. She glues her tiny greenish eggs to the underside of a leaf, and these hatch in about a week. Out climbs—a grotesque caterpillar!

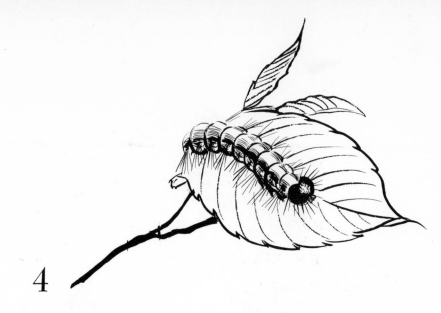

4

. . . and the Beast

Have the eggs of the Monarch butterfly somehow become mixed up with those of an insect monster? Has Beauty produced a Beast? It would appear that she has, for the caterpillar that hatches out is certainly her offspring. Yet it cannot fly and in no way does it resemble the beautiful butterfly. In fact it does not look like an insect at all.

The caterpillar of the Monarch is a food machine. It eats only milkweed leaves, and it would starve before it would nibble on any other kind of plant. It gorges itself, and the only time it stops eating is when it is ready to molt, shedding the skin that its appetite has made too tight. In only two weeks of feeding, it grows from a tiny speck to a fat two-incher. Its rings of black, yellow, and white are warning coloration, for the caterpillar, too, tastes vile to birds.

The caterpillar is perfectly engineered for its only occupation—eating. Its short legs keep its mouth-parts close to the leaves. Its chunky body holds an enormous amount of food.

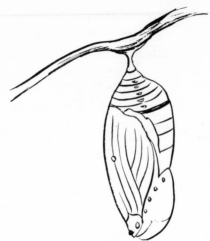

Pupal Case of Monarch Butterfly

Its jaws are sharp instruments for chewing. Everything else has been streamlined out of its design. It has little use for antennae and large compound eyes, so these features are very tiny.

I once captured a large Monarch caterpillar and kept it in a rearing cage, well supplied with milkweed leaves. (The last chapter will show how to make a rearing cage.) After a day it stopped eating. I thought that I had injured it, and that it was dying. However, had I stopped watching the caterpillar, I might have missed one of the grandest shows in nature, for the caterpillar was preparing to change its shape once again.

Slowly, it pulled itself to a twig in the cage, and from its mouth-parts spun a sticky pad of silk. It did a somersault, then attached its abdomen to the wad and hung downwards. After several hours the skin suddenly split open, and revealed what entomologists call the pupal (PEW-pull) case. This case looked like a little greenish house, speckled with round dots of gold which resembled nailheads. It was the "resting stage" of the Monarch, while it prepared to pull new surprises. Butterflies shed their skin to form a pupal case, but moths usually spin silken cocoons.

The *pupa* (PEW-puh), however, is not really resting. Inside the house, changes are taking place. The caterpillar is being dismantled and put together again in the shape of an adult Monarch. As I watched through the translucent walls of the pupal case, I could see the wings developing and gradually taking on color.

In a few days the case split open, and out crawled a bedraggled creature that hung for an hour or two from the empty case. I felt as if I were watching the opening of a flower. The wings began to unfurl slowly, and soon a perfect Monarch clambered on the cage cover and tried to get free. I took the butterfly outdoors and released it, letting it fly off to repeat the curious life cycle of its kind.

I had seen the Monarch follow the entire cycle from a glistening egg to a caterpillar, then to a green house with golden nails, finally to a magnificently colored adult butterfly. The whole process was as amazing as if a bear should go into a long winter sleep and awake as an eagle in the spring.

Insect Double Life

This extraordinary double life of insects is called *metamorphosis* (pronounce it MET-uh-MORE-fo-siss), which means "change of form." Butterflies and moths are the best-known of the insects that change their shapes. But beetles, wasps, bees, and ants also change in much the same way. The Ladybird beetle is the adult form of a wingless little *grub*. The young of the mosquito is a tiny *wriggler* in a pond. The offspring of the fly is a gruesome *maggot*. With all these insects, metamorphosis is said to be "complete."

There are, however, many other insects, such as grasshoppers and crickets, whose young resemble the adults, except that the young lack wings. When the young look like the adults, they are known as *nymphs*, and the metamorphosis is called "simple."

Those insects that display a complete change of shape are the most fascinating to know about. Now for a closer look at the stages through which a butterfly or moth goes.

The *egg* is the first stage. With a magnifying glass, you will be able to see that the eggs have nearly as much variety as the insects themselves. The eggs are beautifully colored in all hues of the rainbow, and they are also interestingly shaped. If you search carefully, especially on the underside of leaves, you may find some eggs. The adult usually fastens the eggs to the particular kind of plant that the young will later feed on.

The second stage is that of the *larva* (LAHR-vuh). Butterfly and moth larvae (LAHR-vee) are called caterpillars, and these larvae more closely resemble worms than they do adult insects. A larva never has wings, and its mouth-parts are designed for chewing. At first, you may doubt that a caterpillar is an insect because it has more than the three pairs of legs. But if you will look closely, you will see that the only *jointed* legs are the three pairs at the front end of the caterpillar body. In addition, there are five more pairs of soft, temporary legs further back on the body to hold up the long "caboose."

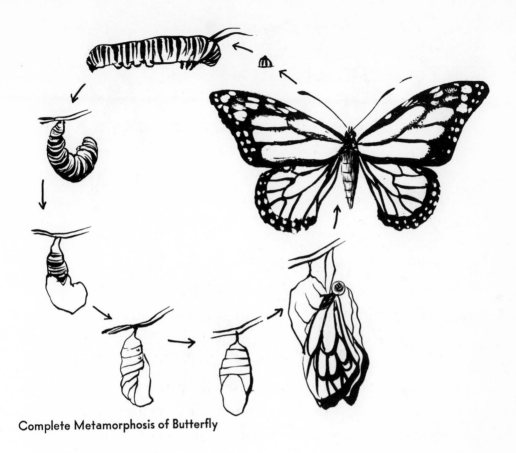

Complete Metamorphosis of Butterfly

Few other creatures are so hungry as caterpillars. The "jump" in the Mexican jumping bean is caused by the caterpillar of a little moth that is eating away inside the bean. During the first three weeks of its life, the caterpillar of a *Polyphemus* (pahl-ih-FEE-muss) moth eats food weighing 86,000 times as much as the caterpillar weighed at birth!

Caterpillar Defenses

How do these soft-bodied caterpillars, lacking a stinger or bite to protect themselves, ever manage to survive? Some are protectively colored, patterned exactly like the leaves on which

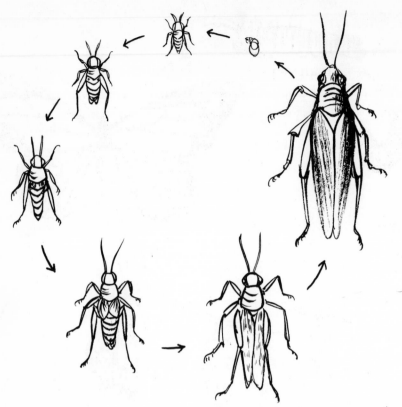

Simple (Incomplete) Metamorphosis of Grasshopper

they feed; others may resemble twigs or bark. Still other caterpillars are clothed in weird colors, as if dressed for a Halloween party. They are ornamented with beads, bristles and horns to scare off birds and sometimes other insects.

The scariest of all the caterpillars is the Tiger Swallowtail. It has two large eyes painted on the top of its abdomen which make it resemble a snake's head. Swallowtail caterpillars are really the skunks of the insect world. They have little slits behind their heads; from these slits they shoot out bright orange horns which give off a nauseating odor. It is believed that the horns protect the caterpillars from bird enemies.

Other caterpillars defend themselves by means of hairs and bristles, which are often poisonous enough to produce a bad rash on a human being, or to irritate the nose and eyes. So be careful not to touch a hairy caterpillar with your fingers.

The Brown-tail moth is a specialist in hairy defenses. The caterpillar is hatched with barbed hairs which are extremely irritating to a human being. When this caterpillar spins its cocoon, it includes some poison hairs from its body. The adult moth then collects the hairs from the cocoon and places them on her eggs. Thus, the hairs protect the moth throughout its life.

The fuzziest caterpillar is the Woolly Bear, the larva of the plainly dressed Isabella Tiger moth. This very common caterpillar curls up each fall for a long winter sleep, as does a bear. Warm winter weather may bring it out of its hiding place, an occurrence that has given rise to the folklore that the Woolly Bear can predict the spring. If you poke at a Woolly Bear, it rolls up into a ball like a porcupine.

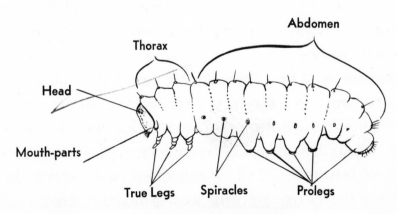

Anatomy of Caterpillar

The caterpillar of the Tussock moth can sometimes be found on city sidewalks on windy summer days, where it has been blown from the shade trees. This caterpillar is dressed in a bright red headpiece, and has four white tussocks on its back which bristle with hairs. You will be lucky indeed ever to see an adult of this moth. The female is the color of bark, and is born without wings. She lives just long enough to mate and lay her eggs.

Cocoon Hunting

The pupal stage is the third in the life of a butterfly or moth. After the caterpillar has grown to its limit, it stops eating and often turns a sickly color. The caterpillar of a butterfly usually sheds its skin to reveal the pupal case, often called a *chrysalis* (KRISS-uh-liss).

Most moth caterpillars, on the other hand, spin cocoons. A large moth may use as many as 1000 yards of silk to make its cocoon. These silken houses give protection against rain and wind. Cocoons may endure temperatures many degrees below zero during the Arctic winter. The ant "eggs" sold by pet shops to feed to aquarium fish are not eggs at all, but really ant pupae in their white cocoons.

Cocoons can best be found during the winter on trees, fences, and among fallen leaves. Cocoon-hunting allows you to rear perfect specimens of the mature moths. Place any cocoons, that you have found, in a rearing cage among dry leaves or moss on top of slightly moist earth. Keep them cold during the winter, and in the spring, you will see the moths emerge.

Woolly Bear Caterpillar and Adult Isabella Tiger Moth

How do the adults get out of their silken cases? It seems as though some caterpillars prepared for that difficulty when they spun the cocoons. They construct little trap doors. Others have a chemical key that loosens the door of the cocoon. A harsh fluid from the moth's mouth weakens the silk so that the adult can climb out.

After allowing its wings to dry, the moth flies off to join the other butterfly and moth jewels. The colors of many of these insects are more striking than the finest patterns that man can paint. Let us look at some of these flying jewels in the Color Guide.

5

Flying Jewels

A Guide to the Color Pictures of Butterflies and Moths

MOURNING CLOAK. This is one of the most familiar of the butterflies in this country and is found both in woodlands and meadows. It is the first butterfly to appear in the spring, the advance guard of all the flying jewels. Mourning Cloak spends the winter as an adult and sometimes flies about on sunny days even in early March, when there is still snow on the ground. It has a wing spread of about three inches, and is one of the most magnificent specimens to be found in any collection. Look for the caterpillars of this species on the leaves of willow, elm, and poplar trees.

PAINTED LADY. This butterfly is probably the most widespread in the world. On its tiny two-inch wings, this hardy creature spans the Mediterranean Sea and flies over the Atlantic Ocean to Bermuda. Its caterpillars feed mostly on thistles, sunflowers, and hollyhocks.

RED ADMIRAL is about the same size as the Painted Lady, and also ranges over much of North America. It is one of the few butterflies to take wing at night. Red Admiral caterpillars usually restrict their feeding to nettles.

TIGER SWALLOWTAIL. The most familiar and largest is 6½ inches in length. It ranges from northern Canada to southern United States. I have even seen these butterflies sipping nectar from window-box flowers in New York City. The caterpillars feed on a wide range of tree leaves, such as wild cherry, tulip, birch, poplar, and others. The Tiger, one of the Swallowtails, is easily recognized because of the "tails" on its hind wings. They like sweets and usually are to be found in any flower garden. Caterpillars of most Swallowtails are insect skunks; they have scent organs to ward off bird attack.

QUESTION MARK. If you look carefully at the underside of its wings, you can detect the curved silver line and dot which give this butterfly its popular name. This is one of the Anglewing butterflies, which are camouflaged by the ragged edges of the wings to resemble dead leaves. Like the Mourning Cloak, the Question Mark passes the winter as an adult. So by poking around in hollow trees, you may also be able to collect specimens in winter. The caterpillars feed on elm and nettle.

COMMA (not illustrated). This species is similar to the Question Mark, but is somewhat smaller and has a different kind of punctuation mark on its wings.

41

MONARCH. This is undoubtedly the best-known American butterfly. On its 3½-inch wings, it has spread around the world to Hawaii, Australia and western Europe, although in many cases it was probably a stowaway aboard ocean liners. The caterpillars feed on leaves of the milkweed family only. VICEROY (not illustrated). This butterfly mimics the color scheme of the Monarch to gain protection from birds, although it lacks the bitter taste of its model. The Viceroy is nearly an inch smaller than the Monarch. It can also be distinguished by its different method of flight: the Viceroy makes quick wing beats, then glides; the Monarch rocks from side to side. You will usually find Viceroy caterpillars on poplar and willow trees.

CABBAGE BUTTERFLY. This is a tiny member, about an inch and a half long, of the White and Sulphur family of butterflies. In fact, the word *butterfly* comes from the color of one of the European Sulphurs. Members of this world-wide family can be identified by their yellowish-orange or white colors. The pattern on their wings is a very simple one. The Cabbage Butterfly was introduced into Quebec accidentally from Europe about one hundred years ago. It has spread across the North American continent, sometimes becoming a serious pest of cabbages.

PEARL CRESCENT. One of the most familiar of the butterflies, the Pearl Crescent is found in open places and along roadsides nearly everywhere in North America. In spite of its small size, which is usually less than one and a half inches, it darts after other butterflies that invade its territory. The cater-pillars are sociable, and many of them often feed together on their favorite plant, the aster.

GIANT SILK MOTHS. These moths are as colorful as butter-flies, and are the largest moths in this country. Their wing spans are often more than half a foot. None of the adults eat, for they emerge from their cocoons with mouths insuffi-ciently developed for feeding. They live for only a few days, just long enough to find a mate and to lay eggs.

CECROPIA (see-KROH-pee-yuh). The largest Giant Silk moth, it ranges from the Atlantic to the Rockies. Its caterpillars feed on a wide variety of tree leaves.

LUNA. This is probably the most beautiful moth. It is pale greenish-white and has long, flowing wings like robes. It is found in the eastern half of the United States and Canada.

PROMETHEA (pro-MEETH-ee-yuh). The most common of the Giant Silk moths. Its cocoons are easily found during the winter: look for a curled leaf hanging from sassafras, spicebush or wild cherry. The leaf is probably wrapped around a cocoon of this moth for protection and disguise.

POLYPHEMUS (pahl-ih-FEE-muss) (not illustrated). This species has a great staring "eye" set on each of its rich brown wings. This is not really an eye but may look enough like one to frighten birds. Once seen, the caterpillar is not easily forgotten. It raises the front part of its body, thus making itself look very frightening, and it clicks its jaws.

HUMMINGBIRD MOTHS. Such a moth drinks nectar from deep-throated flowers, and duplicates the hovering flight of hummingbirds. Many of these attractive moths feed during the day. On the hind part of its body, the caterpillar of a Hummingbird moth usually has a horn, a fearsome-looking instrument that does not sting or harm in any way, but which may scare birds. When the caterpillar is disturbed, it has an additional defense: it rears up, looking much like the Sphinx of Egypt, and for that reason these are also called Sphinx moths. Most of the caterpillars burrow into the ground to construct a tiny chamber, where they change into the pupal form.

PINK-SPOTTED HAWK MOTH. This is among the most beautifully colored of this group and is sometimes found around morning-glory and sweet-potato vines.

STRIPED SPHINX. This species flies at any hour of the day or night, and may be found fluttering around city street lights. Identify it by its green and yellow body, tinged with pink on its rear wings (not illustrated).

6

The Tireless Ants

I once dug up an ant city and transferred the large queen, together with a few dozen smaller workers, to a nest I had constructed. *(See instructions for building an ant nest at the end of this book.)* For months afterwards, I watched the ants act out their fascinating lives.

An Ant Metropolis

The first thing they did in their new home was to set about busily constructing a large room for the queen. The queen is the most important member of the ant city; only the queen lays the eggs that develop into more workers. The workers did not halt their digging until a bedroom had been prepared. The queen remained there, surrounded by her court attendants who fed her, washed her and carried away the eggs she had laid.

The ants seemed tireless in their work. They rushed about, and shifted the soil particles to build more rooms and passageways. They rarely rested until they had laid out the plans for the new city, and construction was well under way. Then their pace seemed to slow down. They even took daytime naps. When they awoke, they stretched as kittens do and immediately set about washing themselves. If you single out one ant in your nest to watch, you will see that it washes itself about every half hour.

Also, the ants appeared to have play sessions. They held sparring matches and rolled over and over as though they were wrestling. They never seemed to hurt one another while playing, although there are few fighters more dreadful than ants when they are in earnest.

When two ants met in my nest, they tapped their antennae together, as if they were talking sign language. Somehow, the ants were able to divide up the tasks of running the city. When I dabbed paint, so that I could identify her, on a worker who was caring for the eggs, I noticed that it was she who always remained with the eggs. Other ants which I had painted with a different color specialized in food gathering.

46

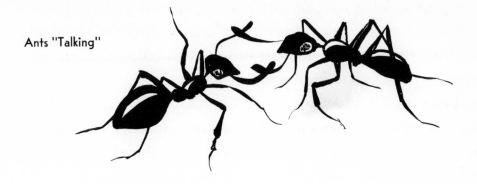

Ants "Talking"

One of the most unusual things to be seen in the nest is how ants feed each other. An ant has two sets of stomachs. One stomach is the receptacle for its own food; the other is a shopping basket where food is stored until the ant returns to the nest. When she does return, she passes the food she has stored into the mouths of the other ants.

As you watch your ant nest, you will realize that ants can achieve amazing feats for such tiny insects. If ants were the size of people, they would be constructing skyscrapers three times as tall as the Empire State Building in New York City. Unlike beehives, no two ant cities are ever exactly alike. Ants use different kinds of architecture for different building sites.

Not only do ants build a year-round nest deep in the soil, but many kinds also construct a summer cottage nearer the surface. Often they erect a high mound of leaves and earth on top of the nest, which heats rapidly and serves as an incubator for the young. Other ants construct mounds, like dams, to keep rain water out of the nest.

Ants are possibly the most numerous and most successful of all insects. A thriving ant city in the tropics may have a population equal to that of a human metropolis. Ants have worked out many methods for survival in this crowded world, and in some ways their societies resemble ours.

There are about 5,000 different kinds of insects and spiders which are guests—some invited, some not—in ant nests. Some kinds of ants carry out dairying operations: they keep insect-cattle which they "milk."

There are even farming ants, which may be found from New York to Florida and Texas. These ants raise their own fungus crops in special underground hothouses. The workers gather bits of leaves which they chew into fertilizer for their gardens. They are expert weeders, and when more crops are needed to feed the growing city, they plant new gardens.

Other ants, found in western United States and Canada, are harvesters of grain. They collect seeds from plants and store them in underground granaries. The powerful-jawed workers serve as threshing machines to break open the tough seeds. Should a heavy rain flood the grain elevators, the ants carry the seeds on the first sunny day outdoors to dry.

Ants do many things that humans do, and they also possess some of man's worst traits. Ants wage costly wars against other ant cities, and they enslave weaker ants. The slave ants then do the work of their masters. Some of the masters have been fed by slaves for so many millions of years that they have lost the ability to feed themselves. If their slaves did not chew the food for them, they would starve in the midst of plenty.

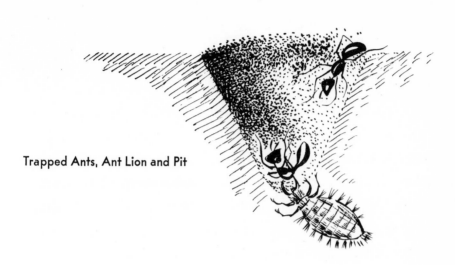

Trapped Ants, Ant Lion and Pit

The Ant and the Lion

The most skillful of ant enemies is the Ant lion, and the
traps that it constructs are usually found near the nests of its
prey. Very few insects make traps, but the Ant lion constructs
a spectacularly successful one. It closely resembles a scooped-
out funnel, and is usually built under overhanging rocks,
porches, or wherever the soil is protected from rain.

The trap is made by the larva of what will become a graceful
insect. But the larva itself is a hunched, ugly creature, with
jaws that look like a pair of ice tongs. Although the Ant lion
is one of the most repulsive of insect larvae, we can still admire

49

the construction of its trap. When a passing ant blunders onto the brink of the funnel, the whole wall collapses under it, causing an avalanche.

The victim tumbles to the bottom where the Ant lion waits —buried, with only its jaws sticking out of the soil. Should the ant manage to gain a struggling foothold on the brink of the trap, the lion loosens the ant's hold by tossing bits of soil at it.

I once dug up an Ant lion and placed it in a large jar of earth where I watched it construct this engineering marvel of a trap. It first backed into the soil, shoving aside the grains and flicking them out of the way with its shovel-like head. Once the rear of its body was safely in the soil, it swung the front part around in a perfect circle. Then it backed up a little more, and revolved in a smaller circle.

In only half an hour, the Ant lion had dug a funnel with steep, smooth sides. In all, it had moved about a cubic inch of earth.

Occasionally, rather large insects stumble into this trap by mistake. They are so quickly overcome by the Ant lion that some entomologists believe that the lion may use poison. For that reason, it is safest to handle Ant lions with a pair of tweezers. After dining on the ant or larger insect, the lion flicks the remains out of the pit and moves off to construct another of these amazing traps.

7

Insects In Armor: Beetles

If we placed in a single line one of every kind of plant, mammal, fish, bird and insect—in fact, all living things—every fifth one would be a beetle. There are more kinds of beetles than there are of any other insect group, and beetles are among the most interesting insects of all.

Beetles can be found nearly everywhere. Some spend almost their entire lives under the bark of trees, while others are water giants that attack frogs and small fish. One of the commonest beetles in the eastern part of the United States is one that arrived here from Japan accidentally. Its young, called grubs, live in the soil, nibbling away at the roots of grasses and some other plants. If you were to dig up only a square foot of soil where Japanese beetles are common, you might find as many as one hundred grubs.

Most insects wear a sort of armor, but beetles are clothed with the sturdiest armor of all. Even their front wings are armored. They no longer use these wings for flying. Instead, the beetles have converted the front wings into a hard sheath that folds over the rear flying wings and protects them. That is why the scientific name for beetles is *Coleoptera* (koh-lee-OPP-terr-uh) which means "sheath-winged."

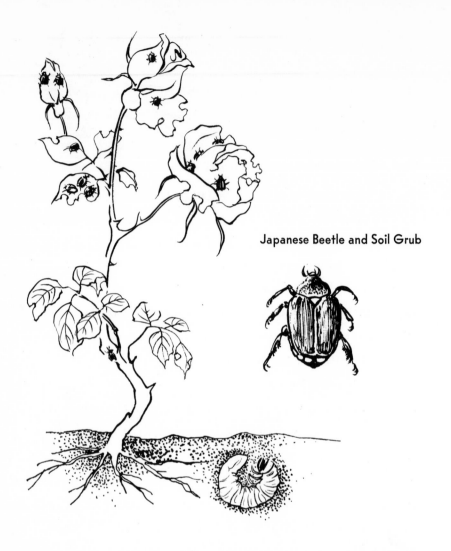

Japanese Beetle and Soil Grub

Beetles are the most powerful living things, ounce for ounce, on earth. One of these little strong men can lift more than 750 times its own weight. Stag beetles, whose jaws have developed into what look like miniature moose antlers, are mighty fighters. Two males will often duel over a female, their giant horns clashing in battle. The Rhinoceros beetle also wears horns, and these horns resemble those of the African rhinoceros.

52

Among the most ferocious of beetle hunters is a Tiger beetle which pursues its prey on its long legs. It is striped like a tiger, and pounces on its prey in the same manner. Once it manages to down an insect with a flying leap, the beetle grasps the victim in its powerful jaws to prevent escape. Take care in handling the Tiger beetle; it sometimes gives a painful nip.

The young of a Tiger beetle is as ferocious as the adult. It lies hidden in a little hole in the earth, with only its head visible. When an insect passes within range, it is caught in the sharp jaws. No matter how hard the victim struggles to escape, the larva cannot be tugged out of its burrow. That is because special hooks on the end of its body anchor it to the sides of the burrow.

Beetles have armored exteriors, but there is also one kind that seems to have a stomach made of iron. This is the Drugstore beetle. It finds red pepper among the easier foods to digest! At least forty-five different drugs and poisons are on its menu. A near relative of this beetle likes the same bill of fare, as well as one other strange food—strong cigars!

Bombardier beetles, which inhabit damp spots under leaves and stones, use their own kind of tear gas. When one of these beetles is threatened, a special organ on the rear of its body sprays out an irritating mist. The protection of this spray usually gives the beetle time to scurry off. But if its pursuer still continues the attack, the beetle can toss a few more bombs.

The Click beetle is an insect acrobat. If you disturb one, it suddenly drops to the ground and plays possum. After a few moments, when the danger has passed, it is ready to resume its affairs. But because it probably had landed on its back, it uses a special instrument on its thorax to right itself—a little lever that fits into a notch on the abdomen. The beetle bends its back and releases the lever, which snaps its body inches into the air. If it once more lands upside down, it clicks again and continues to do so until it can scud away.

An Insect Lantern

Thousands of Fireflies may spark their greenish lanterns above a field on a summer night. Fireflies are not flies at all, but rather they are darkly-clad beetles that lie hidden during the day.

You can quickly learn the knack of catching a Firefly. Carrying your flashlight, watch a Firefly drop down to rest, and keep your eye on the glowing light. Approach close to that spot, then suddenly switch on your flashlight. If you keep the beam shining on the beetle, it will not fly off, and you can easily catch it in your hand. A Firefly is harmless and after a short struggle will soon lie quiet on your hand. It may also resume its flashing and let you watch its performance close up.

You will see that the light produced by the Firefly comes from special segments at the end of its abdomen. The segments feel cool to the touch, for unlike the electric lamp, the light of a Firefly does not give off heat. Inside the segments are a few drops of an unusual fluid known as *luciferin* (lew-SIFF-err-in) which means "light bearing" in Latin. This fluid gives off light. But the beetle lantern needs a switch also, so another chemical turns the *luciferin* off and on.

The beetle lantern is under the control of the insect. If it wants a bright light, it merely breathes in a large supply of oxygen. The oxygen flicks the switch and makes the *luciferin*

Fireflies

glow. As soon as the oxygen supply is cut off, the light goes out. Both male and female Fireflies carry lanterns, which are believed to be of use in finding mates in the dark.

The Ladybird

The Ladybird is the most familiar of all the beetles. If it were not so widespread, people might journey for miles to see its gemlike beauty. There are many kinds of Ladybirds, and all have the distinctive dress of red, orange, yellow or black polka dots.

55

The Ladybird doesn't seem to walk; rather its little legs twinkle like those of a ballet dancer. It is as neat as an ant, and is constantly cleaning itself. After landing, the roly-poly Ladybird can be seen trying to tuck her wings under the wing covers.

Ladybird and its Larva Feeding on Aphids

In the same way that we occasionally leave a shirt-end sticking out of a suitcase, one of her wings is often left untidily outside the closed wing covers.

The bright colors of the Ladybird are as necessary to its survival as are those of the Monarch butterfly. The Ladybird gives off a vile fluid which makes it distasteful to birds. Birds immediately recognize this beetle's coloration and do not attempt to eat it.

Ladybirds often gather in sheltered places in the fall. There they spend the winter, often huddled together in masses of about 2,000,000 insects. When a farmer discovers such a collection, he has found a prize, for Ladybirds are among the farmer's most valuable friends. They hungrily feed on a variety of insect pests.

The farmer often collects the sleeping Ladybirds, keeping them during the winter and then transferring them to his own fields in the spring. Other farmers buy Ladybirds from commercial suppliers just as they would purchase insecticide. Ladybirds are truly "living insecticides."

8

City of the Bees

In order to make seeds from which new plants will grow, a flower must be fertilized, just as an egg must be fertilized. But the male flowers are unable to walk to the female flowers with their fertilizing pollen. So plants have had to evolve ways to transport the pollen. Most trees and grasses send clouds of pollen into the air to be carried by the wind, and perhaps by luck a few grains may land on female blossoms.

Many other plants use a much more efficient method. They grow bright, attractive flowers, like colorful advertising signs, to win attention. They scent the flowers and bait them with sweet nectar in order to attract insects. Insects steal the nectar and much of the pollen, but in doing so, some of the pollen rubs off on their bodies. The pollen is then carried to the next blossom that the insect visits.

Pollen Baskets of Worker Honeybee

Honey Shopping Bag

Wasps, flies, butterflies and moths are all pollinators, but the most famous of such pollinating insects are Honeybees. In fact, Honeybees could not exist without the nectar and pollen they collect.

Without Honeybees, many of our crops would bear neither seeds nor fruit. These insects are so vital to certain crops that in the orchard areas of New York State alone fruit growers rent more than 10,000 bee colonies each year. The hives are loaded on trucks at night when the bees are sleeping inside, and are driven to the orchards to pollinate the trees. The helpful Honeybee is not native to North America. It was brought here by settlers from Europe in 1638, and it mystified the Indians who called it "the white man's fly."

As the bee searches the flowers for pollen and nectar, she darts over the blossoms, her sensitive antennae tuned to the scent. Suddenly, she dives into a blossom, and her yellow-and-black dress now looks as if she had been playing in a flour factory. She stays on the flower only long enough to unroll her tongue to sip up some nectar. She then puts the tools on her legs to work. The combs and brushes scrape the pollen off her body and pass it back to the rear legs. This pair of legs is equipped with shopping baskets which store large amounts of pollen.

The bee then zooms to the next flower. Since her combs and brushes did not remove every speck of pollen from her body, some rubs against the female parts of the second flower. That is how she accidentally fertilizes it. She fills her leg baskets with pollen until they are overflowing, making them look as if she were wearing golden trousers.

Bees from a single hive may visit 250,000 flowers in just one day. To make only a pound of honey, they may have to take nectar from almost 40,000 flowers. The distances the bees fly to visit these flowers may be equal to a trip around the equator. Some bee colonies are so industrious that they can gather enough nectar to manufacture over two pounds of honey in a single day.

We ourselves could easily collect nectar from flowers. But no matter how hard we might try, we could not make honey from it. Nectar is merely the raw material from which bees work chemical magic to manufacture honey.

A bee collects nectar not in its own stomach but in a shopping bag (called the honey sac) similar to the one ants have. Even while the bee flies homeward from the flower, chemicals

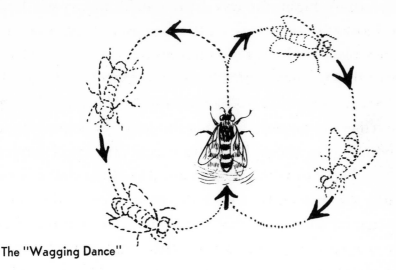

The "Wagging Dance"

in the sac are at work transforming the nectar into honey. Once the bee is back in the hive, excess water is allowed to evaporate, and the thickened fluid soon becomes honey.

Pollen serves a much different purpose. When the foraging bee returns to the hive, she empties her pollen baskets and gives the supply to the young bees. Only the young bees have special chemicals in their mouths, and as they chew the pollen, it turns into a sort of mush, or pablum, used to feed the bee larvae.

Bee Talk

An Austrian scientist, Dr. Karl von Frisch, discovered that bees are able to communicate with each other. Each bee returning to the hive, reports to the other bees on where she was and what she found. She also gives exact directions on how to find the flowers. So precise are her directions that the other bees can

61

make a "beeline" flight directly to the field where she had found the blossoms. How can a little bee give flying instructions about a place perhaps two miles away?

She does this by means of a "wagging dance"—a figure 8, during which she wags her abdomen rapidly. The speed with which she dances accurately informs the other bees how far it is to the flowers. For example, if she makes only eight circles in a minute, that means the flowers are $3\frac{3}{4}$ miles away. The more rapidly she dances, the closer the flowers are to the hive.

The wagging also provides additional information. She wags only at a certain point in the dance, and this gives the other bees the compass reading of the correct direction. The other bees move close to the dancer and wave their antennae about to pick up the scent of the blossoms that she has visited. They thus learn what kind of flower the dancer has been "talking" about. Now that they have full information on which direction to fly, how far to fly and what to look for when they get there, the other bees take off from the hive.

Soon these bees also return from the collecting grounds, loaded with nectar and pollen, to make their report. They dance and win over additional followers to return to the same flowers. So efficient is this method of communication that there is no wasted effort. The bees receive their flying orders, and make a beeline to the flowers.

9
Bee Society

A farmer may have a single dog or a cow or a goat, but he would be unable to keep only one Honeybee. If a bee is separated from the other members of the hive, it soon dies. That is because bees have a social system in which each bee has its own job to perform. Some bees care for the queen, or act as policemen to keep bandits out of the hive. Others make honey or wax or bring back raw materials for food.

Were we to put a bee city to sleep with ether, so that it could be examined in safety, we should be amazed at the vast numbers to be found inside. Populations of 50,000 bees are not unusual, and there may be as many as 75,000. But one of the bees, and only one, would stand out from all the rest. This is the slightly larger queen. She is the mother of all the other bees, the only bee in the entire city that usually lays eggs.

There are a few other unusual bees in the city, also. These are the drones, males with very large eyes and plump bodies. The thousands of other bees are all workers, females that do not lay eggs.

An Insect Bulletin Board

The workers perform the entire task of running the city. Each worker is expert in a particular job, depending upon its age.

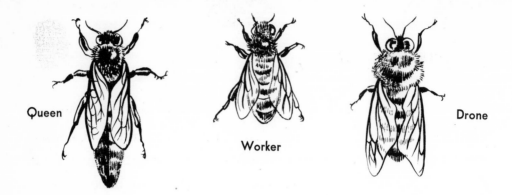

Queen
Worker
Drone

The youngest bees care for the eggs and feed the larvae. This is a tremendous task for a young bee, since each of the larvae may eat as many as 1300 meals a day.

After a week or so of that assignment, the bee switches to another job. It now gives out the wax used to build the honeycombs. Only the week-old bees have a special wax factory inside their bodies. Each of the honeycombs is made up of hundreds of little six-sided cells. Some of these are used as nurseries, others for food storage.

The bee may then clean out the hive, or guard its entrance. Only when the worker approaches the end of her short, month-long life does she forage in the fields for nectar and pollen. The worker bee goes from job to job, just as a camper might follow the list of summer activities on a bulletin board.

A worker, even though she does not lay eggs, possesses an egg-laying mechanism on her abdomen. She uses this mechanism when she stings, and it deposits a droplet of venom, rather than an egg, in the skin. The stinger of a bee is a mar-

Tiger Swallowtail

Cecropia Moth

Promethea Moth

Question Mark

Monarch Butterfly

Cabbage Butterfly

Red Admiral

Painted Lady

Mourning Cloak

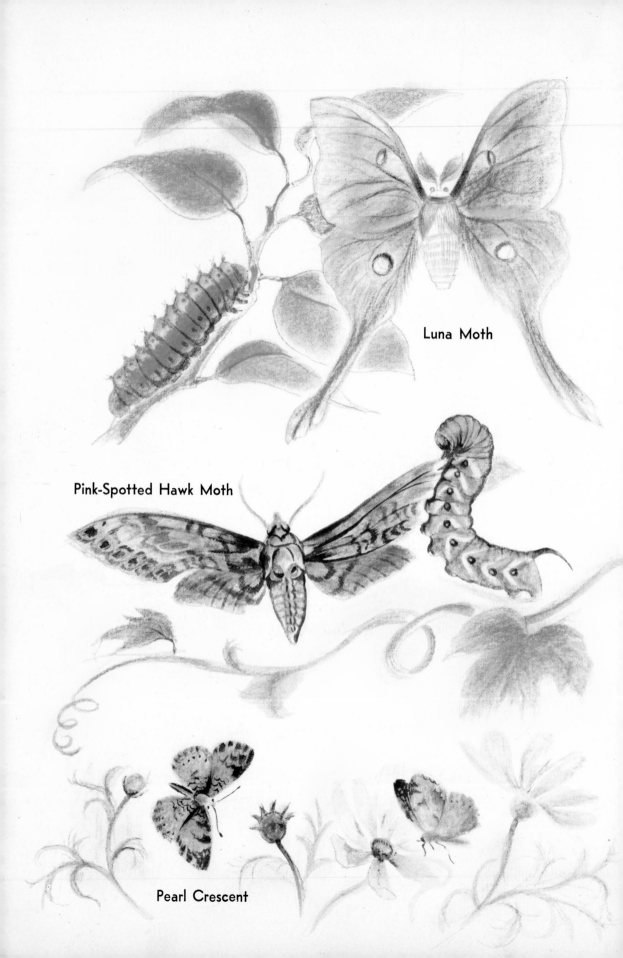

Luna Moth

Pink-Spotted Hawk Moth

Pearl Crescent

velously designed instrument. It has barbs like a fishhook so that it easily slides into the skin, but cannot very easily be pulled out.

When a Honeybee stings, it loses its sting—and its life. The stinger is ripped out of its body, usually with the poison gland still attached. If you are ever stung, do not pull at the stinger, since that will only squeeze more venom into you. Rather, scrape the stinger out of your skin with a needle as if it were a splinter.

Bumblebees and Others

Besides the Honeybee and the Bumblebee, there are about 5000 different kinds of bees in the United States and Canada. They are the solitary bees which have no society of queens, workers, and drones. Usually, a solitary-bee mother digs a burrow in the soil, provisions it with pollen, and lays her egg. She then seals the hole, and flies off to repeat the process, without ever seeing her offspring.

Leaf-cutting bees are among the most fascinating of the solitary bees. A Leaf-cutting mother snips off circles of leaves and flowers to line her nest in the soil. As she speeds back to her burrow with each large burden, she resembles a flying leaf. She lays an egg on the leaves, and places a supply of pollen near it so that the hatched larva can conveniently dine.

Now, on top of that nursery, she constructs another one. She may construct half a dozen of these little nurseries out of leaves, each one containing its own pollen cafeteria for the larvae.

Finally, she is ready to seal the burrow. Amazingly enough, she remembers the exact size of the burrow opening, for she

Leaf-Cutting Bee

flies to a nearby tree and cuts a piece of leaf that is a perfect fit. She keeps adding leaf circles to the burrow until the opening is completely plugged. The burrow may be sealed with a dozen leaves, all of which the bee has cut to size so exactly that they resemble a stack of coins.

The life of a Bumblebee is similar, in some ways, to that of a Honeybee. But there are also many fascinating differences. A Bumblebee does not make her home in a beekeeper's hive or a hollow tree, as does a Honeybee. Instead, the Bumblebee queen searches for an abandoned rodent's nest which she can convert into her underground town.

She does not even bother to redecorate the rodent nest, but goes right to work. She first constructs a little pot, using the wax that pours out of her abdomen, and fills the pot with honey. The Bumblebee queen makes another pot next to it, and lays

66

about eight eggs in it. Like a chicken, she seats herself on top of the pot to brood the eggs.

The larvae are fed honey, stored in the pot, and pollen gathered by the queen. After they spin their cocoons, the queen once again broods them. She may take time off to build another pot and lay more eggs in it, as well as to replenish the supply of honey. The queen has little time to rest until the first young Bumblebees emerge from their cocoons. These are all workers, and they take over the task of feeding the larvae.

The queen now becomes merely an egg-laying machine. Her underground town never grows so large as the hive-city of the Honeybees. The population increases to a few hundred workers only. The queen that founded the town dies in the fall, and so do the workers. Only the young queens survive to found new bee towns the following spring.

Bumblebee

10

Daggers With Wings: Wasps

Wasps are related to bees, and, like bees, also possess stingers. But the wasp's stinger does not have barbs. Instead, wasps' daggers can be inserted again and again. Like Honeybees, some wasps have their own societies, and also erect cities. Hornets hang their nests from roofs and tree branches; Yellowjacket wasps build underground citadels, as Bumblebees do.

Papermakers, Masons and Diggers

Bees use wax from their bodies to construct their honey-combs, but Hornets and Yellowjackets have to make their own paper for their nests. Man must build giant factories with complex machinery to manufacture paper, but the wasps are able to do this with their tiny mouth-parts. First they fly to a rotting fence or a wood pile and scrape off a few fibers with their sharp jaws.

They then chew these splinters and mix them with saliva until the pulp becomes as workable as papier mâché. Next, they mold the pulp into the desired shape, and after it dries, it stiffens into a thin piece of gray paper.

Not all of the paper-making wasps construct teeming cities. The large, black Polistes (po-LISS-teez) wasp often attaches her paper nest to people's homes. This wasp seems to approve of man and his ways, for rare is the country house that does not have one of her nests hanging from the eaves. The Polistes wasp is probably the meekest of all the large wasps, and she does not sting unless she is actually touched or severely annoyed. So you can watch closely her wonderful method of building a paper saucer without being in danger.

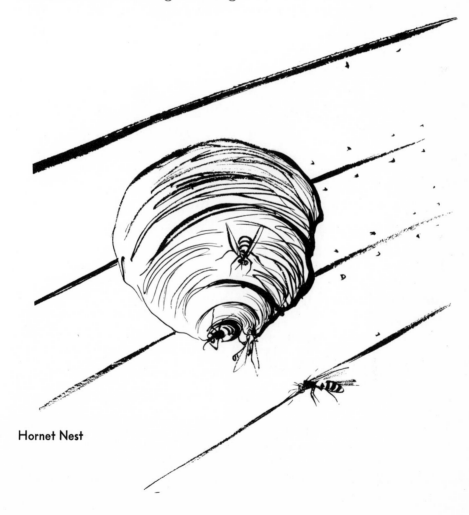

Hornet Nest

The Polistes queen usually spends the winter in a barn or house, asleep in some dark cranny. In the spring she hangs a tiny paper stem from the eaves of the roof, and attaches to this what appears to be an upside-down saucer. The little cells in which she will rear her young hang from the saucer; the eggs are pasted in, so that they will not fall out.

Unlike people, adult wasps feed on a liquid diet only, but the infants eat meat. The Polistes mother kills insects which she chews and feeds to her larvae. The population of her saucer nest rarely exceeds more than a few dozen young. So if we refer to a Hornet nest as a city, we should have to say that the Polistes saucer is only a crossroads village.

If you watch a mud puddle in the summer, you are likely to see wasps landing on it for a moment. These are Mud Dauber wasps that build adobe huts, in the shape of pottery or bullet shells. The mother wasp scrapes together a tiny ball of mud which she carries to her building site. Like a sculptress at work, she keeps adding pellets of mud until she has fashioned a strong, well-turned cell. She stocks the cell with as many as a dozen spiders or caterpillars, which she has stung, to feed the larva when it hatches out. The adobe dwelling is sealed up, and the female then flies off to build another house.

A different kind of wasp, the Ammophila (am-MOFF-ih-luh), is an excavator. She digs out her nursery in the soil. When it is time to seal the burrow, she does something almost unique in the insect world. She examines nearby pebbles, and finally chooses one just the right size to fit her jaws. She uses the pebble as a hammer to pound down the loose soil and close the burrow opening. Ammophila is one of the very few living things, besides man, actually to use tools.

70

Polistes Wasp Nest Under Roof

Plant Houses

On their leaves or branches many trees bear unusual growths that resemble fruits. Sometimes these growths hang like brown apples from twigs; occasionally they resemble little pills attached to the leaves. The growths are called galls, and some of these are the nurseries of tiny wasps.

In late spring, inspect a few oak branches and you will soon find a peculiar brown "apple" hanging from one of the twigs. The brown color tells you that the gall has nearly ripened and that the tiny wasps inside are almost ready to leave their nursery. Keep this oak apple on moist soil in an ordinary drinking

71

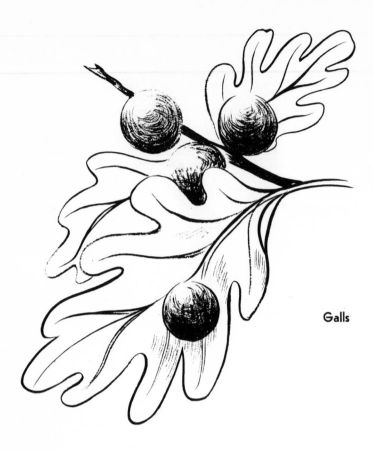

Galls

glass tightly covered with cheesecloth and you will soon find your glass filled with tiny wasps. If you look closely at the gall, you will see pinprick openings; these are the doors that the wasps cut to escape from the gall.

During the winter, the mother of one of these little wasps had climbed over the oak tree, searching for unopened buds. She inserted her egg-laying drill into a bud and laid an egg. While the buds not visited by the gall-making wasp put out their familiar leaves in the spring, the bud containing the egg soon swells into a strange shape. Then, amazingly, the gall is visited by a different kind of wasp, and she lays her eggs in it also!

72

Other insects besides wasps also make galls. There are often two kinds of galls on the familiar goldenrod weed. One looks like a tiny globe, and harbors a little fly.

The other gall is shaped like a tapered rod, and is attached to the stem. This one is made by a small brown moth. The caterpillar of this moth feeds inside the gall until it is ready to pupate. But before going into its resting stage, it must first make preparations for the adult moth to escape from the gall. The adult moth that will emerge from the pupal stage would be trapped inside the gall, since it lacks chewing mouth-parts. The caterpillar solves the problem very simply. It cuts a trap door in the gall, which it then plugs. The adult moth merely has to push the door open and fly off.

Water-striders

11

Insects of Lakes and Rivers

Backswimmers and Skaters

Some of the most unusual insects live in ponds and streams. Primitive man needed many ages to learn how to build a boat, but at least one kind of insect has a boat built into its own body. The back of this insect is shaped like a rowboat, complete with keel. So, a Backswimmer swims upside down, paddling with its rear legs which are flattened like oars.

Whirligig beetles spin around on the surface of the water, as if they were tiny phonograph records. Half of the Whirligig's body is in contact with the air, and the other half floats on the water. This beetle is built like two animals in one. Half of its body is oily, like a duck's feathers, and sheds water. Its eyes, too, work like a pair of bifocal spectacles. The upper half of each eye is designed to give good vision of happenings in the air; the lower half is made for peering through water.

74

A pond has its skaters, also, but these insects don't have to wait until the water freezes over. These long-legged insects miraculously walk on the surface of the water. So expert are they that Water-striders can be found on the ocean surface, in swift rivers and under waterfalls.

Backswimmers

Because its feet are especially designed, the Water-strider does something that most other insects find impossible. Each foot is equipped with a brush of water-repellent hairs. They work much like snowshoes which allow a person to walk over soft snow without sinking in. The Strider uses the rear legs like twin rudders for steering; it uses the middle pair to give it push. And it holds the front legs above the water surface, ready to grasp unwary insect prey.

If you turn over rocks and stones along the shore line, you will usually find insects under them that construct their own portable homes. They are the larvae of the Caddis-fly, an insect closely related to butterflies and moths, but whose young have taken to strange ways. They use their silk to tie together pebbles, bits of sand, tiny twigs, anything from the bottom of a pond. In some Western states, they even use gold nuggets! They carry these trailers around with them as they search for food.

One kind of Caddis-fly has a larva that doesn't construct a camouflaged trailer, but has a better method of getting food. It spins its silk between the leaves of underwater plants to construct a fishing net to catch other water insects!

Insects that live in water still must have oxygen to breathe. They get it in a variety of remarkable ways.

Backswimmers use an aqualung technique: they have special hairs on their bodies to hold bubbles of air from the surface which are then carried underwater. Whirligig beetles store air in special pouches under their wing covers. Some of the large Water beetles are equipped with a tube, like the snorkel on a submarine, which they stick above the water surface to renew their oxygen supply.

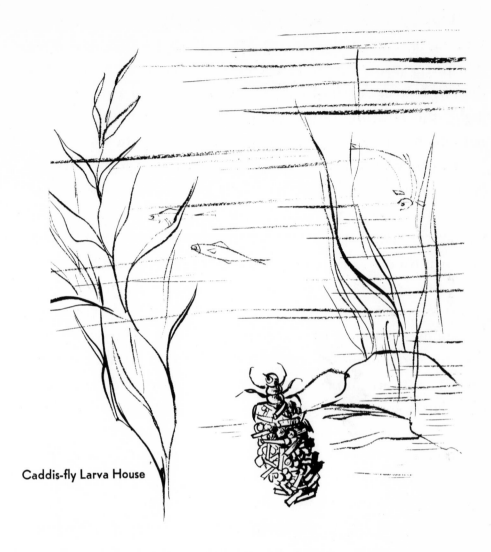

Caddis-fly Larva House

The Darning Needle

The hawks of the insect world, the Dragonflies or "Devil's darning needles," can be found near any lake or stream. In spite of their frightening names and appearance, they are harmless—to people. But to the flies and mosquitoes on which they prey, they must seem like giant, winged dragons.

This insect is adapted for catching insect prey in the air. Its long legs are useless for walking. They are not needed for that purpose anyway, since the darning needle rarely is out of the air. Instead, each of its legs is armed with sharp spines. In flight, the Dragonfly folds its legs into the shape of an aerial net which it uses to scoop other insects out of the air.

In order to spot prey while flying at high speeds, Dragonflies possess probably the best sight in the insect world. The enormous eyes cover practically the entire head, like a football helmet. Dragonflies are also among the very few insects that can turn their heads as we do, scanning everywhere for prey.

Their wings are equipped with an unusual arrangement of muscles not found in most other insects, and with these, Dragonflies can maneuver at high speed. They soar, zoom, and dive like agile fighter planes. All food is eaten on the wing, for these insects are so perpetually hungry that they do not waste time landing to eat a leisurely meal. These giant flying ma-

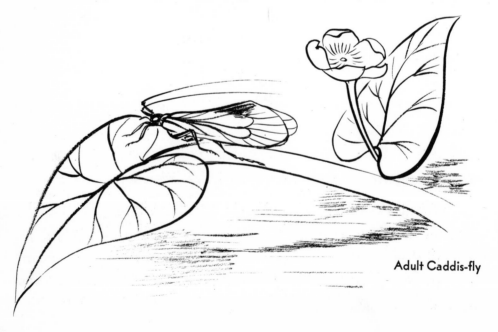

Adult Caddis-fly

Damsel fly (Left) and Dragonfly

chines have enormous appetites, and Dragonflies can gobble up more than their own weight in insects in an hour.

They attack any other insect that flies too close, even large wasps and members of their own kind. When prey is netted in the leg basket, a Dragonfly tears it apart with its sharp rows of teeth. Scientists have named these insects *Odonata* (OH-doe-NAY-tuh), which means "toothed."

During the rare times that a Dragonfly rests, its wings remain outstretched like those of a huge bomber. There is a smaller relative of the Dragonfly, called the Damsel fly, which does fold its wings like the wings of a plane on an aircraft carrier deck.

The outstretched wings of the Dragonfly are a characteristic of primitive insects. And truly the Dragonfly we see today does come from an ancient family. Fossil specimens of these insect pioneers show that they lived in the steaming jungles of ancient vegetation, when coal was first being formed. In those days, millions of years ago, some Dragonflies had wing spreads of nearly three feet, and were probably the largest insects that ever lived. The largest Dragonfly today, however, does not measure more than eight inches from wingtip to wingtip.

Dragonflies lay their eggs in water, and their young live out their lives like fish. To lay its eggs, a Dragonfly skims over the water surface like a torpedo bomber. It occasionally dips the end of its abdomen into the water and jettisons a clump of eggs. The insect that laid these eggs was as striking as a hummingbird; its wings glistened with gold or azure. But what hatch out of the eggs are insect monsters.

The larvae, called nymphs, are mud-colored creatures that hide in the bottom muck or among the water weeds. They move sluggishly, when they bother to move at all. But they are capable of short bursts of speed when pursued by an enemy. That is because they use jet propulsion: they have gills from which they can shoot out water, thus propelling them for a few inches.

How can such a slow-moving monster manage to capture living prey? The nymph has been provided with a unique food-getting tool. Its tremendous lower lip is like an arm, tipped with sharp spines, that shoots out. An insect, or an occasional tadpole, that might carelessly swim too close is grasped and

80

Dragonfly Nymph

pulled into the nymph's hungry mouth. When the lip is not in use, it folds up and covers much of the nymph's head like a mask.

The nymph may live in a pond for two or three years. Then it gropes its way up the stem of a weed until it is above the water. There is a sudden shuddering and the skin of the nymph splits, revealing the hidden beauty of an adult Dragonfly. After half an hour, the wings stiffen—and the submarine has turned into an airplane!

Sundew

An Insect-Eating Plant

12
Insect Oddities

Music Makers

The insect clan has its own orchestra that plays fiddles and beats drums. The music may not sound much like that of a symphony orchestra, for each insect knows only one tune, the same tune that its ancestors have been playing for millions of years. The insect is born with the musical instrument as part of its body, and it never has to take a music lesson.

The best known insect instrumentalists are the crickets. The male Field cricket doesn't use his wings for flying, but rather for playing his violin. On the underside of the front wings he has rows of tiny ridges, like the strings of a violin. The scraper, or bow, is a vein located near the base of the wings. When the Field cricket wants to make music, he merely draws his scraper back and forth over his violin strings.

The violin of the cricket has a sort of loud-speaker attached to it. The wing covers act on the same principle as a sounding board. That is why this insect, only an inch long, can make music that is heard for nearly a mile.

Field Crickets

Field crickets can often be coaxed out of their burrows in a meadow and kept in a rearing cage. The captured insect will live happily on moist bread, lettuce, and especially bits of apple and melon. He will sing his heartiest on warm days. So if you have captured a Field cricket, place his cage in the sun during chilly weather to lift his spirits.

Entomologists call the cricket's method of making music *stridulation* (STRIDD-yew-LAY-shun) from a Latin word meaning "to creak." And creaking is just what a cricket's music sounds like, as if with each chirp a rusty door were swinging. Some grasshoppers also creak. Their bows are located on their rear legs which they rub over the wing violins.

The master creaker of all is another cricket whose incessant singing through the summer night makes it the insect musician most often heard. Although its chirping is well known, the Snowy Tree cricket is rarely seen. It is one of the most beautiful of all insects, having a ghostlike body, nearly white, to which gauzy wings are attached.

Amazingly, a Snowy Tree cricket keeps a regular beat with the rest of the cricket orchestra. The first few crickets that start to play early in the evening are like an orchestra tuning up. But they all soon fall into the same rhythm and manage to keep perfect time throughout the night.

The warmer the weather, the more frequently a Snowy Tree cricket chirps. Those who know the secret can tell the temperature by listening to this cricket. If you count the chirps in fifteen seconds, and then add forty to that number, you will know approximately the temperature outdoors.

The Katydid is cousin to the grasshopper, but he has a different method of playing in the insect orchestra. His fiddle is on one wing; his bow is on the other. When he folds his wings and then rubs them sideways, he produces a rasping sound.

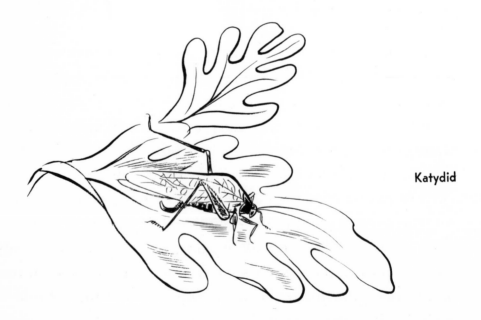

Katydid

Cicada

During the summer a single Katydid may draw his bow a total of 50,000,000 times. Like the Snowy Tree cricket, a Katydid is a good temperature indicator. One method is to count the number of calls per minute, add 160, and then divide by three.

Dr. Robert Snodgrass, presently of the U.S. National Museum, once noted an astonishing fact about the Katydid's song. In the vicinity of Washington, these insects sang a clear *kay-tee-DID*. But in New England, Dr. Snodgrass found that some of them slurred over the song, making it sound more like *kay-DID*. So it seems that insects from different parts of the country may have regional accents just the same as people.

The insect orchestra also has its drummers. These are the male Cicadas (sih-KAY-duhs) and they may be heard beating their kettledrums during summer days. The drums, which are actually tough membranes, are located beneath the wings. The "drumsticks" are thick muscles that pull against the membranes. A Cicada outperforms a human drummer: it may beat its drums 480 times in a single second.

Finally, no orchestra would be complete without the wind instruments. Certain bees, flies, and moths can use their mouthparts in the same manner as a flute is played, forcing air through them and producing a high-pitched note. There is even a xylophone player, for one kind of beetle knocks its head against wood to produce a mysterious tapping.

A Back-Yard Dragon

A Praying Mantis can remain absolutely still on a shrub for hours, its front legs raised toward the sky as if it were praying. However, its legs are not uplifted because it is a devout creature. Rather, they are held that way to seize insect prey instantly, for the Mantis is probably the most blood-thirsty creature on six legs. It snaps up any insect it can find, and is even known to catch an occasional frog or a lizard.

Praying Mantis and Egg Case on Twig

The front leg of the Mantis is fashioned like the blade and handle of a pocketknife, and on the inside of the blade are sharp spines resembling those on a rosebush. These spines are very efficient weapons. Edwin Way Teale, the famous naturalist, once photographed a battle between a Mantis and a venomous Black Widow spider. The first time the Mantis shot out its forelegs they snapped closed on the spider.

Mantises make excellent pets. One day in late summer, my wife found a Mantis on our balcony, eighteen floors above a New York City street. The insect had probably been blown there by a windstorm the day before. She fed it bits of chopped meat, and the Mantis soon learned to drink water from a medicine dropper. After a meal, the Mantis washed its face and thoroughly cleaned its antennae. It soon became so lazy that it ignored the flies hovering near by and awaited the free meal.

As the cold weather approached, we brought the Mantis into the house, keeping it in a shoe box covered with wire screening. We had placed some leaves and twigs inside the box to make the insect comfortable. One day we were amazed to see something that looked like shaving cream flowing out of the Mantis's abdomen onto a twig. The cream soon hardened into a tough covering for the eggs which the Mantis had laid inside the froth.

The female Mantis died soon after that, but we kept the egg case, which had turned a brownish color, all winter. One spring day we saw our rearing cage swarming with green specks. Under the magnifying glass, we could see that these specks were perfect replicas of the adult Mantis—complete to the praying forelegs.

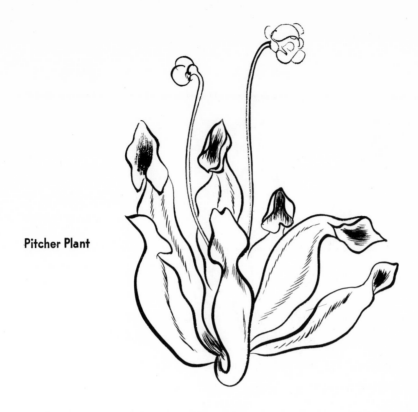

Pitcher Plant

We quickly took the cage to a nearby park and dumped the little Mantises into the shrubbery so that each might go its own way. For, like the adult of the species, a baby Mantis is forever hungry—and not above eating its own kind.

Insect-Eating Plants

Although a great many insects feed upon plants, there are actually a few kinds of plants that gobble up insects. These insectivorous (IN-seck-TIVV-uh-russ) plants, as they are called, have developed wonderful traps. Some use a sort of flypaper; others make use of spikes or slamming doors. A trapped insect rarely escapes and it is digested in the plant's watery "stomach."

Venus's-Flytrap

The most spectacular insect eater is the Pitcher plant. Its trap is made from a leaf shaped somewhat like a funnel with an umbrella over it. There may be half a cup of watery liquid inside the funnel. Like a flower, this trap attracts an insect by means of scent. The unwary insect, following the scent trail over the brink of the pitcher, suddenly slides down its smooth sides as if on a roller coaster. It drops into the deadly liquid, and is used for food by the Pitcher plant.

The Venus's-Flytrap, a plant found only in North Carolina, makes the most elaborate snare. This snare is like two doors hinged together and ready to snap shut on any insect that blunders inside. The signal for the doors to close is given when an insect touches trigger hairs inside the trap.

Although these traps usually mean certain death to most insects, one kind of wasp uses a Pitcher plant as its nursery. First it must drain the Pitcher of its deadly liquid. So the wasp cuts a hole in the bottom, letting the water run out. Then it lays its egg inside and provides the larva with stung caterpillars.

The maggot of one kind of fly leads an even more exciting life. It is born on the outside of a Pitcher, and immediately after birth, it appears foolish enough to slide down the roller coaster into the liquid. But the plant's digestive juices are not powerful enough to penetrate this maggot's very resistant skin. So it crawls about the bottom of the pitcher, feeding on the insects that the plant had captured for its own use!

Millipede

13

Too Many Legs

We learned in an earlier chapter that all insects have their bodies divided into sections, that they wear their skeletons on the outside, and have jointed legs. Insects share these same characteristics with an immense number of other small creatures, such as spiders, crabs, Daddy longlegs, millipedes and centipedes. All of these related animals are called *Arthropoda* (ar-THROPP-uh-duh), a term made up of two Greek words meaning "joint" and "legs."

Spiders come close to being insects, but they don't quite make it. Instead of the three body parts of the insects, spiders have only two. The head and thorax are fused in spiders. They have four pairs of legs, one pair more than insects. Nor do they possess wings, for of all the Arthropods (ARTH-ruh-podds) only the insects can fly.

But some spiders have made up for their lack of wings by learning how to fly with kites. Research airplanes have towed nets at 5000-foot altitudes and many spiders were found among

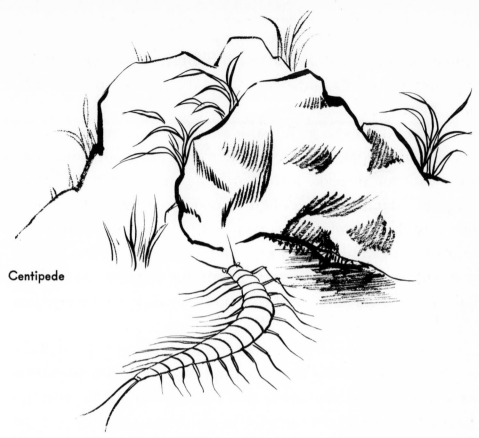

Centipede

the creatures collected. How did those wingless spiders rise nearly a mile into the air?

The Spider's Web

Spiders can put their silk to a variety of uses, one of which is for constructing kites. The young spiders climb to the tops of fence posts and shrubs. They send out long lines of silk which are soon caught by the air. When the tug from the silken kites becomes strong enough, the spiders cast off and are pulled into the air. They may float for hundreds of miles, occasionally landing on ships in mid ocean.

Caterpillars spin silk from an organ near the mouth-parts, but a spider's silk comes from three pairs of tubes on its abdomen, known as spinnerets. With these organs the spider can spin an invisible line as fine as a millionth of an inch in thickness, or it can spin a line so heavy that it can snare snakes, birds, and mice.

I once watched a spider spin a perfect web, and wondered what would happen if I were able to carry enough clothesline rope with me to make a web in proportion to my size. How large would it have to be? I figured that to start my web, I would climb to the roof of a skyscraper and tie my rope to the water tank. Then I would let out rope and descend to the street. Now I would have to run to another building about a block away. I would scale the outside of that building also, stretch my rope and fasten it tightly.

By this time I was exhausted from thinking of all the work and danger involved if I were to duplicate the accomplishments of a little spider. And there are thousands of other intricate lines that a tiny spider can spin in less than an hour.

Not all spiders spin webs as a means of capturing insects. There is a Water spider that uses its silk to bind together dead leaves so that it can sail down streams in its own canoe. Another spider, sometimes found in city parks, uses its silk in a different way. It climbs to the end of a twig, spins out a line and weights it with a ball of sticky silk. When an insect wings past, the spider hurls this line at it like a lariat.

Spiders are shy creatures, usually most active at night, so we often do not realize the vast numbers of them around us. But one scientist set out to count them, and he found over 2,000,000 spiders in a single acre of meadow.

Practically every spider is provided with a poison gland which secretes venom to kill prey or for defense. But only a few of the spiders we are likely to find in North America have

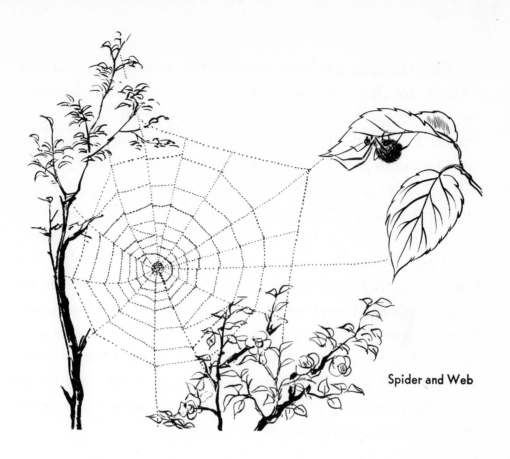

Spider and Web

venom powerful enough to harm us. Some of the large taran-
tulas (tuh-RAN-chew-luhs) of the Southwest can give painful
bites. The only other spider we should avoid is the shiny, long-
legged Black Widow. It can be identified by its single bit of
color, yellow or red, in the shape of an hourglass on its underside. Most other spiders secrete very weak venom. In fact, they
are so timid that they rarely attempt to bite.

Daddy Longlegs

The amusing Daddy longlegs has four pairs of legs like a
spider, one pair too many to make it an insect. Nor is it a true
spider, since it lacks spinning organs to make silk.

This creature has long slender legs, resembling hairs. If a Daddy longlegs grew until its body were the same size as a human being's, its legs would then be about forty-five feet in length. Daddy longlegs can usually escape from enemies by taking giant steps. Even if a pursuer catches it by one of its legs, it is still safe. It merely gives a tug—and the leg breaks off. Later on, it grows another leg.

The body of a Daddy longlegs is so small that it looks like a tiny seed. Examine the body through a magnifying glass and you will see that the eyes are located on a little platform on the creature's back, giving good vision all around it. Also, notice how the "knees" of the long legs are much higher than the body, thus allowing it to hang suspended only a short distance above the ground. In that way it does not have to reach very far to prey upon the little aphids (AY-fidds). We shall learn about them in the following chapter.

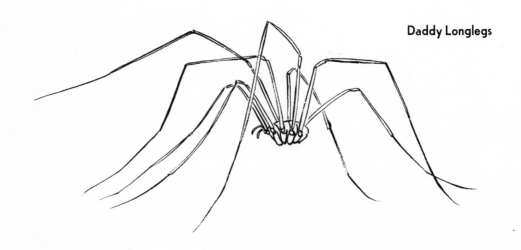

Daddy Longlegs

14
The Web of Life

We have seen how one insect hunts another, how some insects feed on plants or are themselves the prey of plants. No insect, or any other life on this planet, can exist by itself. Nature is like a vast web in which each form of life is linked by invisible threads to many other forms. If we were to pull out one of the threads from our web—that is, completely to eradicate any form of life—many other threads in the web would also come loose. Scientists call this study of the relation of living things to the world around them *ecology* (ee-KOLL-oh-jee).

Let us select one of the humblest of all insects, an aphid, and see some of the threads which attach it to the web of life.

The Lowly Aphid

An aphid is a minute green insect, shaped much like a pear. Actually, it is a living pump. It spends its life sucking the sap from plants and giving off sweet honeydew. An aphid may spend its entire life on stems or leaves, piercing the plant with its hollow beak. Here is Thread I: an aphid is linked to plants because it feeds on them.

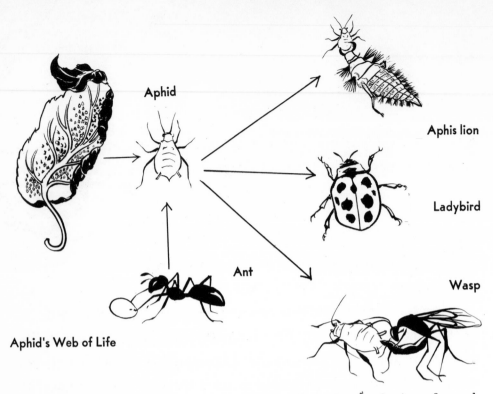

Aphid

Aphis lion

Ladybird

Ant

Wasp

Aphid's Web of Life

This little insect is utterly defenseless. Its body is soft and it wears no stiff armor; it neither stings nor bites. How does it manage to survive? For one thing, it reproduces at a fantastic rate. But it also has formed a remarkable partnership with certain kinds of ants. Many aphids have become the insect cattle of the dairying ants, and in return are protected by them (Thread II).

If you look closely at a colony of aphids on a rosebush, you will probably see ants patroling near by. These ants are the ranchers, ready to give battle to rustlers. Some ants actually build corrals of mud around the aphid herd. When one pasture becomes too heavily grazed, the ants move the aphids to another one. They even gather the aphid eggs in the fall and store them in an underground barn. In return, an aphid produces a golden droplet of honey whenever an ant taps it with its antennae.

98

Friends and Enemies

Many other insects are woven into the life pattern of an aphid. The watchful ants cannot fend off all attackers, and many insects eat their way through the closely packed aphids like a whale plowing through a school of shrimp. Daddy longlegs is particularly fond of aphids and stuffs itself (Thread III). Many birds clean off whole twigs of them (Thread IV). The Ladybird beetle, both in the adult and larval forms, feeds to its fill on aphids (Thread V).

But the most ferocious insect to prey upon these cattle is the Aphis lion (Thread VI). It is the ugly larva of one of the most beautiful of all insects, a Lacewing. A Lacewing seems to fly on wings of wispy green gauze; its eyes are the color of pure gold. The female searches out aphid colonies and lays her eggs near by. A greedy dragon hatches out and immediately sets to work gobbling up the aphids at the rate of about one a minute, hour after hour.

Aphids also serve as living nurseries for some tiny wasps (Thread VII). Rather than construct a burrow or adobe hut, as many other wasps do, these lay their eggs right on the aphid. That way, the wasp larvae do not have to search for a meal when they hatch out.

These are seven of the threads in the life web of an aphid, but there are more, for the insects and birds which feed on aphids are themselves linked to other forms of life. For example, the wasp that lays its eggs on aphids has its own eggs attacked by yet another kind of wasp! And the Ladybirds themselves fall prey to Assassin bugs that have found tiny chinks in this little beetle's armor.

We could even imagine many more threads. The Daddy longlegs which fed on the aphids might itself fall prey to a bird. The eggs of this bird might be eaten by a snake, and that snake might be killed by a hawk. When the hawk dies, it will fall to the ground—and be eaten by some insects. These insects will also die and provide fertilizer for the plants—perhaps the same sort of plants on which that original aphid was feeding!

Thus, throughout the living world no form of life stands alone. As you watch the insects, see how their lives are tied to one another and to other living things around them. Soon you will discover many ways in which we, too, are tied to the web of life. For the plant that the lowly aphids suck dry may be the very one that we want to raise for our own food.

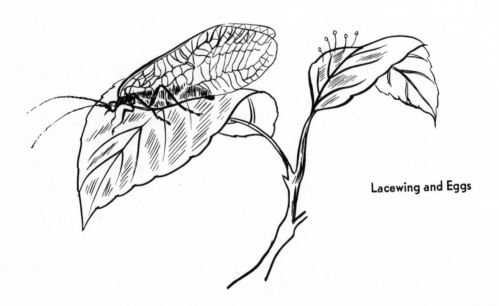

Lacewing and Eggs

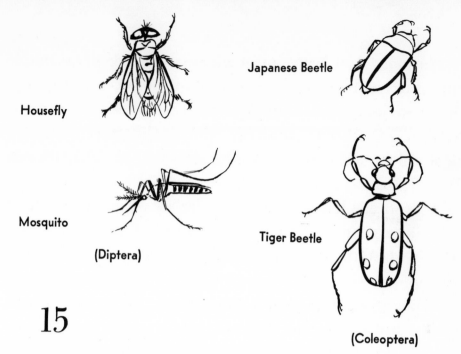

Housefly

Japanese Beetle

Mosquito

(Diptera)

Tiger Beetle

(Coleoptera)

15

Learning More About Insects

Guide for Identifying Insects

In this book we have called practically every insect by its nickname, and we have already learned how very confusing nicknames can be. A Dragonfly is not really a fly; neither is a butterfly, nor a Firefly. Also only certain insects may be called "bugs."

Scientists must be certain that they are all talking about exactly the same kind of insect, so they have given each insect its own scientific name. These names are written in *italics*. Many of them are derived from Latin or Greek words or have Latin endings.

Many of these names may seem to be difficult to pronounce at first. But we have already used parts of scientific names without experiencing too much difficulty, such as the *Polistes* and *Ammophila* wasps.

101

Not only does every insect species have its own scientific name, but entomologists have also classified insects into groups so that we can know about each one's relatives. For example, the Tiger Swallowtail butterfly is the only insect *species* in the world to have the name *Papilio glaucus* (pap-PILL-ih-yoh GLAW-kuss).

This species has a few very close relatives, and they join to make up a *genus* (JEE-nuss), the plural of which is *genera* (JENN-uh-ruh). The Tiger Swallowtail belongs to the genus *Papilio*.

Many genera that appear to be similar compose a *family*. So all of the Swallowtail butterflies make up the family Papilionidae (pap-PILL-ee-ON-ih-dee).

A number of different families are then combined into an *order*. There are more than twenty-five orders of insects. All butterflies and moths belong to the order Lepidoptera.

Finally, all of the orders together make up the Class Insecta which includes every insect known.

When you look up the description of an insect in one of the Field Guides, which are listed at the end of this chapter, you will find the exact scientific name of the insect as well as information about its close relatives.

These are the main orders of insects:

Coleoptera (koh-le-OPP-terr-uh) are the beetles. There are about 27,000 species of beetles in the United States and Canada, more than any other insect order. Identify Coleoptera by the hard pair of outer wings that form the protective cover and meet in a straight line down the insect's back. Beetle young, called grubs, somewhat resemble caterpillars, but they lack the temporary legs on the abdomen.

102

Diptera (DIP-terr-uh) means "two-winged." This order includes the flies and mosquitoes. They make up the second largest order to be found in the United States and Canada, with 17,000 species identified. Many of them are so tiny, however, that you often do not realize the great variety of Diptera that exists. Only insects with one pair of wings are included in the Diptera. Although some other insects have the word "fly" in their common names, like butterfly, Dragonfly, and Damsel fly, they have *two* pairs of wings and thus do not belong in this order.

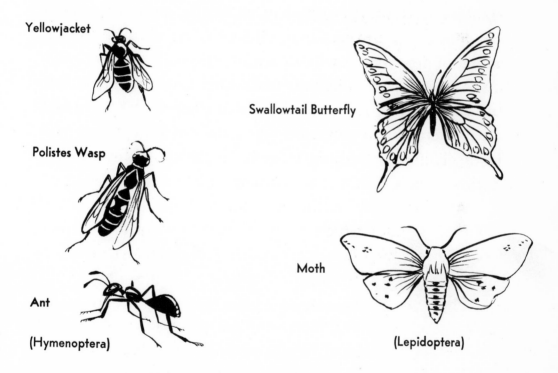

Yellowjacket

Polistes Wasp

Ant

(Hymenoptera)

Swallowtail Butterfly

Moth

(Lepidoptera)

Hymenoptera (HI-men-NOPP-terr-uh) include some of the most fascinating insects on earth—the bees, the wasps, and the ants. There are about 15,000 species in the United States and Canada. Their two pairs of wings look as if they were cut from transparent cellophane, thus giving this species their scientific name, which means "membrane-winged." The majority of these insects sting, so treat them all with respect.

Lepidoptera (LEPP-ih-DOPP-terr-uh) are "scale-winged" creatures—butterflies and moths. Almost all the insects in this order have colored scales on their wings. There are about 11,000 species in the United States and Canada. Their larvae are the familiar caterpillars.

Hemiptera (he-MIPP-terr-uh) include the only insects that can correctly be called "bugs." These all have hollow spears, as part of their mouth-parts, to suck up liquid food. The scientific name of this order means "half-winged," because the inner half of each wing is usually tough and colored; the outer half often thin and transparent. There are about 9,000 Hemiptera in the United States and Canada, including Water-striders, Backswimmers, Aphids, Cicadas, and the Bedbug.

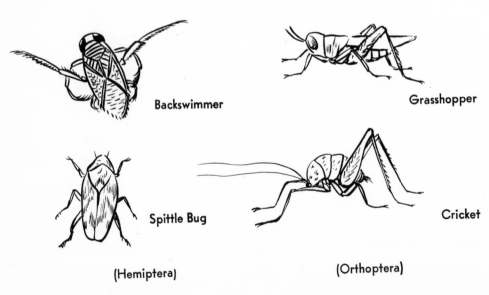

Backswimmer

Grasshopper

Spittle Bug

Cricket

(Hemiptera)

(Orthoptera)

Orthoptera (or-THOPP-terr-uh) are the grasshoppers, crickets, katydids, and roaches. Most of the insect musicians belong to this order. The young lack wings yet they resemble closely the mature insects. There are nearly 1,000 species in this order in the United States and Canada. A related order is the *Mantodea* (man-TOE-de-uh) which includes the Praying Mantis.

Odonata (OH-doe-NAY-tuh) is the order composed of the very ancient Dragonflies and Damsel flies. Their young (nymphs) live in water. About 500 species of Odonata can be found in the United States and Canada.

Neuroptera (new-ROPP-terr-uh) are the lions of the insect world, for this order includes the Aphis lion and the Ant lion. Their adults, though, are among the most beautiful insects in the world. They closely resemble the Damsel flies, but have smaller eyes. Their thin, gauzy wings have earned this order the scientific name Neuroptera, which means "net-winged."

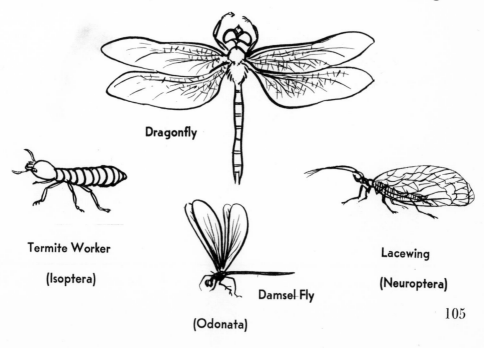

Dragonfly

Termite Worker

(Isoptera)

Damsel Fly

(Odonata)

Lacewing

(Neuroptera)

105

Isoptera (eye-SOPP-terr-uh) are the termites, of which there are about forty North American species. They can be seen only rarely, at the time the winged kings and queens fly out of the soil or wood to go on a mating flight. All American termites feed on wood which they are able to chew but not digest. Therefore, each termite carries in its stomach protozoa (pro-toh-ZOH-uh), microscopic one-celled animals, which digest the wood for them. Termites are often confused with ants. It's easy to tell the difference for an ant has a thin waist between the thorax and abdomen, and a termite does not. Another method of identification comes from the scientific name of this order which means "equal-winged." The front wings of ants are longer than the rear wings.

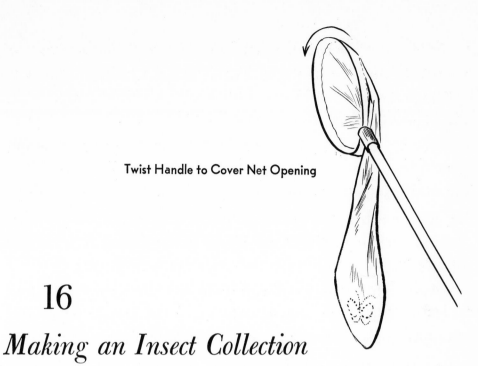

Twist Handle to Cover Net Opening

16
Making an Insect Collection

Collecting insects is an exciting hobby. Of course, not even professional entomologists attempt to collect all the hundreds of thousands of insect species. Some specialize only in certain orders or families of insects. Others may try to collect a specimen of every kind of insect found in one small locality.

Here are a few general suggestions and hints to start you on your collection. Later on, you may want to read some of the books and pamphlets listed at the end of this chapter to learn more about making an insect collection.

Insect Net: This is necessary equipment for collecting most flying insects. There is one simple trick that you should practice before setting out into the field. Once you have captured the insect inside the net, give the handle a quick twist. This action flips the bag over the mouth of the net, closing it and keeping the insect imprisoned in the lower end.

When you see someone chasing an insect and beating the air wildly with the net, you can be certain he is an amateur collector. Stalk your insect until you are within range of it, then make a clean, quick sweep with the net.

Killing jars: A killing jar must be made of heavy glass and have a tight-fitting cover. You will need two pint-sized jars—one with a large opening for Lepidoptera and one with a smaller mouth for most other insects. The reason for keeping Lepidoptera in a separate jar is that some of their scales might rub off and spoil specimens of other kinds of insects.

Although professional entomologists use stronger poisons in their killing jars, you should use ethyl acetate. Ask your druggist to obtain some for you. It is probably the safest substance you can use for this purpose, but if it is not available, buy a bottle of Carbona cleaning fluid. Take care not to breathe the fumes deeply or to spill the fluid on your skin.

Stuff the bottom of an ordinary grocery jar with wads of cotton and pour some ethyl acetate on it until it is saturated. Do this just before setting out on your collecting trip. Then cover the cotton with a piece of blotter, cut to the circular shape of the jar bottom, so that the insect will not come into direct contact with the liquid poison.

It is fairly easy to transfer most insects directly from the net into the killing jar. To prevent a butterfly or moth from marring its wings by beating them, merely give the insect a pinch slightly to the rear of the head. After a few attempts, you will soon learn how tightly to squeeze, so as to stop the beating of the wings.

With a stinging or biting insect, it is a good idea to work it down to the bottom of the net, and then place the end of the net in the killing jar for a few moments. This stuns the insect so it can then be removed in safety from the net and placed directly into the jar.

Even though an insect may appear to be dead in the jar, after a few minutes, it should be left there for at least an hour. Many insects are extremely difficult to kill, and there have been cases of their reviving while being mounted.

Tweezers enable you to handle delicate insects more easily. When taking butterflies or moths out of the killing jar, always use tweezers to avoid rubbing off the scales. As soon as the insect is dead, remove it from the jar and place it between layers of cotton in a box, so that it will not be damaged on the way home. With butterflies and moths, slip each one into its own envelope and keep the envelopes in a box to prevent crushing. Always carry an assortment of various-sized envelopes with you when you are collecting.

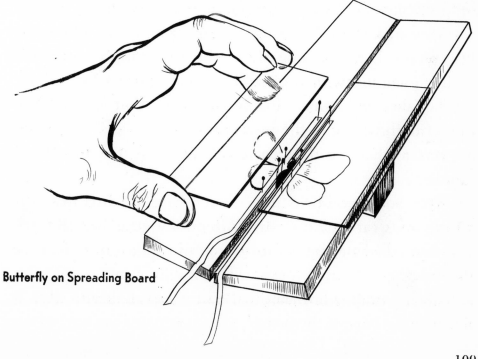

Butterfly on Spreading Board

If you mount your insects as soon as you get home, you will save the step of putting them in a *relaxing jar*. But if you can't do the mounting right away, put a wet sponge in the bottom of a quart jar. Cover the sponge with a wad of cotton so that the insects will not touch the water. Put your specimens in the jar, cover it with cheesecloth to absorb any moisture that condenses, and put on the lid. Leave small insects in the relaxing jar for a day; larger ones up to three days. Insects left too long in the relaxing jar will become moldy.

Most insects can then be prepared for *mounting*. To pin your specimen, first try to visualize where two imaginary lines on the insect would cross. One line goes from the insect's head to its abdomen, and the other across the middle of the thorax. Insert the pin a little to the right of the spot where these imaginary lines cross. Be sure to use only special insect pins that can be purchased inexpensively from one of the biological supply companies listed at the end of this chapter.

Also, stick the pin through a label which tells where the insect was collected and by whom, the date of capture, and the kind of plant it was feeding on. The more information you put on the label, the more valuable your collection will be. You can write the name of the insect on the label later, when you are certain that you have correctly identified it from a Field Guide.

Keep your specimens in a *storage box,* which is made by gluing thick cardboard to the bottom of a cigar box. Pin the insect and the label to the cardboard lining of the box. To keep the box free of insect pests which might want to eat your specimens, wrap a few mothballs in cheesecloth and glue it inside to a corner of the box.

To display the open wings of a butterfly or moth is a much more complicated job. The wings must be extended to remain open in your storage box, so you will need a *spreading board*. It is made of two pieces of wood that meet at a very slight angle, with a thin groove between them to hold the body and legs of the insect. You can make one yourself out of wood or thick cardboard, or you may purchase a board very inexpensively.

Take your butterfly from the relaxing jar with tweezers and pin its body through the thorax to the groove of the spreading board. Then, keep the wings open by pinning two long, thin paper strips so that each one presses against a pair of wings near where the wings join the body.

Now stick a pin behind the strong vein on the front wing of the butterfly, and pull it towards the head into its natural position. Do the same thing with the rear wing. Tighten the thin paper strip, so that the wings will remain in place.

Do the same thing with the wings on the other side. Strips of glass, such as old microscope slides, gently placed on the wings will prevent curling. The specimen should be left on the board for about five days. It will then be dry enough to mount in a storage box.

Insect mounting is a lengthy operation. That is why you will not want to catch and preserve every insect you see. If you did, the results of only an hour's collecting might keep you busy for months mounting specimens. So before you swing your net too often, look first for the unusual or strikingly beautiful insects.

17

Keeping An Insect Zoo

A collection of active insects, caged in your own home, can be more exciting to watch than the sleepy animals to be found at the zoo. Also, many of the interesting and unusual things that insects do can be seen only if you keep them under observation in cages.

Some insects thrive in captivity; some others do not. The most important thing to remember is that in your cage you should try to duplicate the natural conditions under which you collected the insect. If the beetle you captured, for example, was living under a rock, then you can be certain that this insect likes darkness and moisture.

Feeding Tips: **Many** insects are very particular about what they eat. After you have captured an insect that you want to add to your insect zoo, it is wise to look up its name in a Field Guide to find out what kind of food it prefers.

You might begin your zoo with crickets and katydids, since they eat nearly anything that a person does. Moist bread, salad vegetables, or bits of fruit are excellent for them.

One of the biggest mistakes you can make is to water your insects too much, another is to keep them in direct sunlight or near a radiator. A few drops of water a day added to the sand in the cage is usually enough. If water collects on the side of the jar, that shows that you are giving them too much water.

Most insects need some drinking water. You can make a combination water fountain and moistener by using the tiniest bottle you can find. Wrap some cheesecloth around a piece of cotton and stuff both into the bottle. Then soak the cotton until it is thoroughly wet. The water will rise from the cotton to the top of the cheesecloth where the insects can reach it.

Cages: **Many** insects, particularly those that fly only infrequently or not at all, are easily kept in large preserve jars. Fill the bottom of the jar with a few inches of sand. Then cut a hole in the jar cap, and snip off a round piece of wire screening to fit inside.

Such cages are excellent for beetles, crickets and katydids. Use the same sort of housing for Mantises, except that the jar for this insect should be a half-gallon size to give these larger insects more room. Also provide a few large twigs for the Mantis to climb on, and be certain that the sand in the jar is kept moist.

Keeping Spiders: Each spider requires its own cage, since they are all cannibals. The simplest method is to pour an inch of sand into the bottom of an ordinary drinking glass. To prevent the spider from escaping, tie cheesecloth around a large wad of cotton and stuff it into the mouth of the glass. Add a few drops of water to the sand every day.

Most spiders can live for long periods without eating, so you need not worry about daily feedings. A *live* caterpillar or a small fly about twice a week should keep the spider well fed. You will want to provide more space for those spiders that spin large webs, so that they can display their art. A small, square goldfish bowl, covered with wire window screening, does very well for these spiders.

Rearing Butterflies and Moths: Your chances of capturing a caterpillar and watching it develop into an adult are excellent. A simple rearing cage can be made by filling a large flowerpot with loose topsoil. Roll up some wire screening into a cylinder, slightly smaller than the diameter of the flowerpot. Push the cylinder a few inches into the soil. Then cover the top of the cylinder with glass. Keep the flowerpot in a deep saucer so that the soil can be moistened easily by pouring water into the saucer.

This kind of cage provides for those moths that pass their "resting" or pupal stage in the soil. In case you have a caterpillar that suspends its cocoon or pupal case, stick a long twig a few inches into the earth. The twig is needed also, when the butterfly or moth emerges from the pupal stage; these insects often hang from a twig while their wings dry.

To feed the caterpillars, gather a supply of fresh leaves, making certain that you pick the kinds of leaves the insects

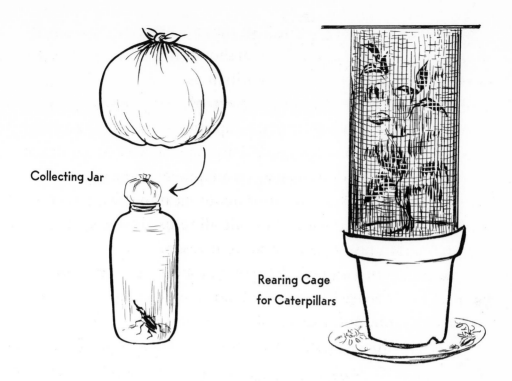

Collecting Jar

Rearing Cage
for Caterpillars

were feeding on when captured. Put the stems into a tiny bottle
of water to keep the leaves fresh, and stuff the mouth of the
bottle with cotton to prevent the caterpillars from falling in.
Lift the wire cylinder and push the bottle into the earth. After
the caterpillars have eaten all the leaves, remove the bottle and
refill it with fresh leaves and water.

When the caterpillar has reached the end of its larval stage,
it may stop eating and grow very sluggish. This is your hint
that it is about to go into its resting stage. Leave the cocoon or
chrysalis in the cage so that you can watch the adult butterfly
or moth emerge.

Do not try to keep the adult imprisoned, as it will soon mar
its wings by beating them against the cage. You can now add
the adult to your collection—or you can mark its wings (with

model airplane paint that has been thinned out) and release it in your garden. If you should see this butterfly again, you would then be able to identify it as "yours."

Making An Ant Nest: Many kinds of ants can easily be kept in captivity. If you capture the queen also while collecting them, then your colony may survive for years—and you can watch the complete development of the ants from eggs to adults. Don't be concerned about cleaning the nest, because the ants do it for you. They pile all refuse in one of the chambers, from which you can remove it easily.

To make the nest, you need two sheets of glass, about the size of this page, and four pounds of heavy plaster of Paris. Lay one of the sheets of glass on a table and, after mixing the plaster thickly, model it to form a series of figure 8's on the glass. Leave the center of each 8 free of plaster, and be sure that all of the centers are connected by passageways. The plaster when modeled should be about ½" high. Then press the second sheet of glass firmly on top of the plaster to make sure that there are no gaps through which the ants might escape.

After the plaster has hardened, remove the top glass and carve out the chambers and passageways more elaborately with a knife. Now wash and dry both sheets of glass thoroughly.

It is a good idea to chill the ants before you transfer them to the nest. Merely put your tightly sealed collecting jar in the refrigerator for about an hour. By doing that, the ants will become sluggish, and can be dumped into their new quarters with little fear of their escaping.

When you are not watching the ants, cover the glass with a sheet of cardboard to keep the nest dark. Decide which chamber you will use for food, and be sure to place it always in that

116

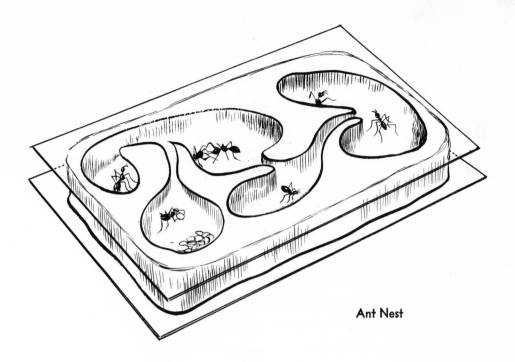

Ant Nest

one. A small, soft-bodied insect, such as a caterpillar, and a few grains of sugar given the ants every two days will keep them well fed. About once a week feed them three or four drops of honey. Remove any uneaten food as it soon spoils. It is easy to keep this kind of nest moist. Merely sprinkle water on the plaster until it is thoroughly wet, once a week in summer and every two weeks in winter. To tend the nest, push the top sheet of glass aside.

Some species of ants may be able to bore through the plaster, so as a safeguard, fill a large baking pan with water. Stand four drinking glasses upside down in the water and place the nest on top of them. Even if the ants do get out of the plaster, they will not cross the moat.

117

Within a short distance of practically every reader of this book is a natural-history museum, a state college or an agricultural experiment station. Many of these places have excellent insect collections which are often on display. Also, many professional entomologists devote hours of their spare time to aiding amateurs. But do not consult the entomologists until you have secured as much information as possible yourself. Entomologists are very busy people—with three-quarters of a million insects to worry about!

After you have kept a few insects in captivity, you will work out your own special tricks. You will soon become expert at bringing insects back alive—so that you can watch close up the most fascinating creatures with whom we share the earth!

18

Books About Insects

Field Guides: The longer you observe insects, the more impatient you will be to identify them according to genera, or even species. A good Field Guide is essential to do this.

Field Book of Insects by Frank E. Lutz, published by G. P. Putnam's Sons in many revised editions, has been the standby for decades, and is the most complete.

The Insect Guide by Ralph B. Swain, published by Doubleday & Co., Inc., 1952, is, however, more attractive looking and easier to read. Many amateur entomologists like to have both books.

For identifying butterflies amateurs and professionals alike use Alexander B. Klots's *Field Guide to the Butterflies*, published by Houghton Mifflin Co., 1951. About 250 species are illustrated in color, and the book gives you practically all the information you need to identify, collect and rear butterflies.

As your knowledge increases, you may want to perform the difficult task of identifying immature insects. The best guide to this is *How To Know The Immature Insects* by H. F. Chu, published by William C. Brown Co., 1949.

Collecting and Rearing: There is so much to this phase of insect study that even experienced collectors can still learn new tricks. Two pamphlets will give you most of the basic information: *How To Make An Insect Collection,* published by Ward's Natural Science Establishment and *Collection and Preservation of Insects.* U.S. Department of Agriculture Miscellaneous Publication 601, and available for 25¢ from U.S. Government Printing Office, Washington 25, D.C.

The Department of Insects and Spiders, American Museum of Natural History, New York 24, N. Y. has printed seven free leaflets on many phases of insect study. These publications give excellent details on making and using insect nets, keeping a collection, rearing live insects.

General Books: Hundreds of excellent books have been written about insects, so it is only possible to list a few of them here. However, I have enjoyed the following books very much, and they usually can be obtained from public libraries. Perhaps you may also want to purchase copies for yourself.

A Lot of Insects by Frank E. Lutz, G. P. Putnam's Sons, 1941

American Social Insects by Charles D. and Mary H. Michener, D. Van Nostrand Co., Inc., 1951

Ant World by Derek W. Morley, Penguin Books Inc., 1953

Dancing Bees by Karl von Frisch, Harcourt, Brace and Co., 1955

Freaks and Marvels of Insect Life by Harold Bastin, A. A. Wyn, 1954

Grassroot Jungles by Edwin Way Teale, Dodd, Mead & Co., 1944 or revised edition

Hunting Wasp by John Crompton, Houghton Mifflin Co., 1955

Insect Fact and Folklore by Lucy W. Clausen, Macmillan Co., 1954

Insect World of J. Henri Fabre ed. by Edwin Way Teale, Dodd, Mead & Co., 1950

Insects in Their World by Su Zan Swain, (Garden City Books), Doubleday & Co., Inc. 1955

Insects Their Ways and Means of Living by Robert E. Snodgrass, Smithsonian Institution, 1930

Insects, Yearbook of Agriculture, U.S. Government Printing Office, 1952

Junior Book of Insects by Edwin Way Teale, E. P. Dutton & Co., 1953 or revised edition

Lesser Worlds by Nesta Pain, Coward-McCann, Inc., 1958

World of the Honeybee by Colin G. Butler, Macmillan Co., 1955

19

Pronouncing Index